A
UNDER A
SPELL?

The Master Plan Revealed

Ambassador Ausar

Edited by Nubia Gonney

MW00935821

Table of Contents

Dedication

This book is dedicated to the memory and legacy of my immediate Ancestors.

Uatu Nasir Gonney , Cousin Kevin Oneil, Cousin Kimmy, Grandfather Irvin Oneil, Grandpa Allen, Aunt Josephine, Uncle Craig Gonney, Aunt Patsy, Uncle Louis Ford, Aunt Dorita, Aunt Maybelle, Aunt Viola, Great Grandma Emma, Uncle Benny, Uncle Yarick, Uncle Rudy, Uncle Fred, Linda Sheard, and Michael Jones.

Special Acknowledgements

My beautiful children Isis, Uatu & Amari, My Queen Nubia, My Mom, My Dad, My sister Aquabah, Grandma Oneil, Grandma Bananas, Uncle Mark, Aunt Miata, Aunt Linda, Aunt Yvonne, Uncle Calvin, Aunt Robin, Aunt Barbara, Aunt Paulette, Aunt Paula, Uncle Kelly, Brothers in Law Corey and Ibn Sheard, Grandma Sheard, Grandpa Sheard, Aunt Wynn, Uncle DJ, Uncle Phillip, Aunt Gladys, Aunt Coreen, Aunt Vanessa, Cousin Lawerence, Cousin Sologne, Cousin Britney, Cousin Dwayne, Cousin Tia Brown, Cousin Crystal, Cousin Simion, Cousin Zaire, Cousin Paulette, Cousin Michaela, Cousin Lucy, Cousin Tyrese, Cousin Tanzi, Cousin Terrance, Cousin Jada, Cousin Lamont, Cousin Raymond, Cousin Alfredo, Cousin Carlos, Cousin Greg, Cousin Valerie, Cousin Desiree, Cousin Doris, Cousin Gregory, Cousin Kenny Boy, Cousin Shelby, Cousin Joseph, Cousin Joel, Cousin Patrick, Cousin West, Cousin Diane, Cousin Koran, Cousin Kiara, Cousin Kofi, Lance Harris, Patrick Manswell, Christopher Wilmore, Big Dev, Marc Cunningham, Gavino, Trevor Mitchell, Trevor Mitchell Jr., Karim Valdes, Ronnie, Steven Gills, Brian Jenkins, Basir, Robert Martin, Steady Eddie, Lynn, Fitzgerald Watson, Jason, Sha,

Cashawn Myers, Queen Tyese, Baba Cordell, Angela Fairwell, Sharonda Glover, Jamar Glover, Mr. & Mrs. Glover, Jaren Glover, Kinya Travis and family, Raymond & Keisha Burr, Lisa Creech and family, Entire Lefferts Place family, Mrs. Smith, Kenny Smith, Eddie Smith, Evelyn, Junior, Candace, Hector, Jose, Jetty, Tony, Justice, Tiz, Freedom, Azar, Milton Moy, Andy, Kevin Dinkins, Nandi Black, Kojo Black and entire family, Tee, Bunny, Ira and entire family, Pops @ Joloff, Nancy Jackson, Aaron, Alton & Key, Phil and brothers, David, Mr. & Mrs. Harris, Marisol, Omar Morris and family, Woody, Juanita Dunbar, Guess, Kent Taylor, Maurice Mo Money, Ademola, Jack Brown, My Irvington N.J. family, Ivan Carter, Brian Carter, Sean, Mike Q, Vinnie Q, Henry McNair, Harvey Dock, Rodney Daniels, Valerie Hester, All my facebook family, All my blogtalkradio family, Dr. Phil Valentine, Moorish Science Temple, Dr. Muata Ashby, Nation of Gods and Earths, Hebrew Israelites, Nuwaubian Nation, Nation of Islam, Yoruba community, all traditional Afrikan spiritual systems, Ra Un Nefer Amen and Ausar Auset Society,. Thank u all for your inspiration, support and love given in your own unique way!

Introduction

The concept of this book was born in 1999 as I traveled through New York City observing people around me and how they interacted with me and others. During that time I began to carry around a small pad and wrote notes on a daily basis to better understand what was distracting me from achieving spiritual greatness. I know the word "spiritual" is a buzz word for some and a religious trigger for others; however, I was not involved in any particular religion at the time I began this writing. I had completely divorced the idea or notion that "God" exists exclusively inside of some particular faith, denomination, belief system, or religion. I used the term "spirituality" to describe not a mystery God in the sky sitting on a throne as some man, but as a galvanizing force/reality that links us together in ways that are tangible and intangible. Religion, for me, did not serve its stated purpose to my people and mankind in general. It seemed up for question as to its involvement in our disunity, apathy, and confusion. I would start my day out in a positive mood intentionally, wanting to see what things were happening around me and within me, that attacked the positive state I was in and wished to remain in. I recorded my mood changes, emotional fluctuations, and the things people did or said around me that had the potential to cause a positive or negative distraction. The most intricate details were captured in this little notebook pad, which I wrote the time and date on every entry. I was like my own behavioral scientist doing an experiment on myself. I still have that original pad with me.

During this time I didn't research material on what I was dealing with, because I was too busy solving the unknown equation within myself, seeking to uncover *why* we get emotionally and mentally distracted or thrown off course from maintaining peace of mind. This is why the book is written as a conversation without too many references from other books. Truthfully, I didn't use other books to write this book –the content of this book and the revelations therein is derived from self dialogue. Because of the personal nature of this writing, it took some time for me to publish it. I did update and omit things for 2010, building on what I was saying in that little pad in 1999. This book came from my heart and my love for my people not as a tool to divide or cause hatred for anyone else.

This book is a user-friendly manual into the realm of the mind. Take your time and analyze these findings for yourself and build on what I wrote and apply the wisdom if you so choose. I still carry a pad with me most of the time to jot down my findings or insights life brings into my awareness on a moment by moment basis. In conclusion, there exist a tremendous amount of distractions bombarding our psyche at any given moment. These distractions are so unique to each individual in terms of what triggers them to respond or become distracted that it is difficult to pin down what's going on exactly with each person or what prevents individual progress or peace of mind. This book is an attempt to do that. I am not a "Christian" by title but after writing this book it seems that "Paul" in the New Testament was on to something when he spoke about the battle not being against flesh and blood, but against principalities and other unseen forces. This is not a mystery God theory or "spookism", but a very real observation coming from someone unbiased and unafraid to look deep into the causation of events. There appears to be much we do not see, recognize or accept about this reality we are currently experiencing.

I know some of you when you read this book are going to say, "I thought that only happened to me" or "So that's what that means." I encourage you all to write me and let me know how this book matches with your unique experiences and let us open up the dialogue on this hypnotic state we all should be trying to break free from. Peace and love to you all. May our children, and their children's children, inherit a better world because of the things we addressed and dealt with in our lifetime without fear.

Understanding Key Terms

What is a "Spell"?

According to Webster's New World Dictionary the definition of the word "Spell" is:

1. A word, formula, or form of words thought to have some magic power; incantation.
2. Seemingly magical power or irresistible influence; charm; fascination
3. A trance- cast a spell on; to put into, or as into, a trance… under a spell, held in a spell or trance; enchanted.

What is a "Trance"?

M.E. < Old French "transe", great anxiety,
fear < transir, to perish < Latin "transpire",
to die, literally, go across: see Transit.

1. A state of altered consciousness
   somewhat resembling sleep,
   during which voluntary
   movement is lost, as in hypnosis.
2. In spiritualistic belief, a condition
   in which a medium passes under
   the control of some external force,
   as for the transmission of
   communications from the dead
   during a séance.

What is an "Incantation"?

Latin "incantare" < in- (intens) + cantare: see Chant

1. The chanting of magical words or formulas that are supposed to cast a spell or perform other magic.
2. Words or a formula so chanted.

What is "Enchant"?

M.E. "enchanten" < Old French "enchanter" < Latin "incantare", to bewitch < in- (intens) + cantare, sing:

1. To cast a spell over, as by magic; bewitch.
2. To charm greatly; delight.

What is "Fascinate"?

Latin "fascinatus" fascinare, to bewitch,
charm < "fascinum", a charm < akin to
German "baskanos", sorcerer.

1. orig. to put under a spell; bewitch.
2. To attract or hold motionless, as by a fixed look or by inspiring terror.
3. To hold the attention of by being very interesting or delightful; charm; captivate.

What is "Charm"?

M.E. "charme" < Old French < Latin
"Carmen", song verse, charm < "canere", to
sing: see Chant.

1. orig. A chanted word, phrase, or verse assumed to have magical power to help or hurt; incantation.

2. Any object assumed to have such power, as an amulet or talisman.

3. Any action or gesture assumed to have magic power.

4. A quality or feature in someone or something that attracts or delights people.

5. Verb tense. To act on as though by magic; seemingly cast a spell on. To attract or please greatly; enchant; allure; fascinate; delight.

What is "Chant"?

French < Latin "cantus", song.

1. A song or melody.
2. A simple liturgical song in which a string of syllables or words is sung to each tone.
3. A monotonous tone of voice; sing song mode of speaking.
4. Anything uttered in this way, To say something monotonously or repetitiously.

Further Understanding A Spell

A spell is a repetitive thought, suggestion or feeling activated in the subconscious mind through chanting, songs, prayers, monotonous speech or words spoken, and actions performed, that resonate to the conscious mind purposefully or unknowingly to generate an automatic response or future response in the "victims" thinking and/or behavior. A spell is cast into the subconscious thought pattern and manifests itself as habits, cravings, longings, desires, needs, and control parameters. Control parameters are created by spells cast because once under a spell of enchantment, your thinking becomes temporarily captivated, thus your behavioral responses are easily predictable and controlled. Let's analyze the key terms defined to get a more practical understanding of what a spell is, how it works and the words associated with it.

Webster's New World Dictionary defined the word **"Spell"** as a word, formula, or form of words thought to have some magic power. So according to the definition of spell, just one word can be said to be a spell. Words such as: War, God, Devil, Death, Sex, Violence, Racism, and Religion, for example are all one word concepts that can and does act on the mind and body, because as the definition states, these words are "thought to have some magical power". The power in each of these words are thought by most people to have meaning and power over their lives and other people's lives, thus by definition these are spell words! You see, we have been trained and taught to attach "magic" power

13

to these words since we were babies. So now, these words as adults have the ability to put us in a trance like state when they are uttered or spoken repetitiously. Do not let the word "magic" throw you off mentally. This word "magic" is a spell word like the other words listed, as it causes an immediate response upon hearing this word. Magic is simply the unknown or unexplained source of power that influences your thoughts and behavior. This word does not have to be thought of in terms of Disney or Harry Potter's magicians and sorcerers, or some movie using magic as a theme with all the production. In fact, magic is an enchantment that is designed to fascinate your mind and have you mesmerized by some action or word. Webster's definition also mentioned magical power as an irresistible influence or charm or fascination with someone or something. Just think about your favorite television show, movie, sport, actor, or entertainer and how they seem to have an irresistible influence over you watching them perform. During their performance you are actually spellbound and placed into a trance. Think about that! That has nothing to do with a scary movie, yet it has a tremendous unseen and unanalyzed influence over your life when you become enchanted or spellbound by the things that entertain you.

Is being under a spell wrong? I can not say that all enchantments are wrong, since you can be placed under the influence of a positive force or positive words, thus being under a "positive spell" for lack of a better term. The problem is most of the spells we are currently under are *not* positive, but dangerous, divisive and destructive.

Being placed under a spell is how all these blood sucking corporations earn their living. They have behavioral scientist on their payroll assisting their marketing team on how to enchant their audience into buying their product. The difference between what these major corporations do and what your local mom and pop businesses cannot do is afford to influence your thinking and behavior on a grander scale through the television medium via commercials and advertisements. These major corporations also use subliminal advertisements in which they insert ideas and their product brand directly into your subconscious mind and bombard your psyche nonstop. Remember repetition is the key in casting spells, and nothing is more repetitious than all these commercial advertisements seen on television or heard on the radio. These corporations advertise their product, which is usually garbage to begin with or not good for your health or longevity, while you are watching a program you like. So they sneak in the backdoor of your mind so to speak while you are transfixed on another "program" which is casting its own spell on you! These commercials subconsciously enter your mind and then masquerade itself as **your** desire, want, or need. Do you see that? You assume your not being influenced by the fast food, car, jewelry, and clothing commercials because you may think you are aware of what they're trying to do or because you may turn away the moment your program is interrupted by these commercials. Or you may think because you get on your cell phone or computer or talk to someone during these commercials that you're not being hypnotized. The fact that you're not paying active attention to these commercials actually works more in their favor to subliminally influence you, because now you're being influenced without your conscious mind involved to refute or challenge the message. You can watch a fast food commercial and consciously challenge their claims to actually be healthy or real meat products and thus diminish their influence somewhat by being consciously aware or you can ignore them and be subconsciously influenced by their advertisements. Because you didn't challenge their claims consciously, the mind accepted their claims and now transformed itself into a desire, want, or need that you erroneously believe is your own. Now you want that product or find yourself thinking about that product or find yourself looking for ways to get it or feel you really need it. That's spell casting 101.

Now can you see how dangerous all these television "programs" and commercials really are? You would literally have to battle every single commercial image and concept presented into your mind consciously in order to fight the spell being cast. Are you really ready to do that every time you watch television? Are you ready to do that every time you listen to the radio? Like in a war or fight, the minute you drop your guard for a second you make yourself vulnerable to be attacked and defeated. Our minds are being constantly and consistently bombarded by spells, suggestions and influence to control our thinking and thus our behavior.

According to the definition of the word **"Trance"**, it is a state of altered consciousness resembling sleep during which voluntary movement is lost, as in hypnosis. Where did the hypnotist conduct his work in the beginning of Western Psychology's hypnotherapy—on a couch? And where do you sit motionless in which your voluntary movement is lost and your in an altered state of consciousness—on a couch watching television! Whenever we sit in front of a television we are being hypnotized and placed in a trance state. Once in this trance like state, in which our consciousness is altered, spells or suggestions can be placed in our minds that affect and influence our thinking and behavior in very predictable ways.

Now we look at the words *incantation* and *chant*, which are other vehicles or modes in which spells are cast. In Webster's definition, **incantation** is the chanting of magical words or formulas that are supposed to cast a spell. These are known phrases that are shown to be effective or bring about the same effect repeatedly. Notice Webster used the word "supposed to" in his definition. This word is used to cast doubt on the validity of the concept, even though the definition exists and evidence of its validity has been documented. This same **validation of concepts** are used in Webster's dictionary when it puts the name of Bible characters inside its book, but does not use doubt words which may question both the validity and historicity of these characters. However, when discussing other ancient religions much older than Christianity and its characters or "gods", they use terminology to denote them as being myths, legends, folklore or lower case g for God! Why? Because they are casting a spell of Christian religiosity, or Christian supremacy on you, so you will accept the supposed reality of the Bible and its "God" over another cultures deity and its "god". Look up for yourself the names of Bible characters in the dictionary and see how they are defined as historical men and women even though no proof outside of the

21

Bible exists. Now look at the definition of Krishna and notice how they define it. Krishna is defined as: Sans "krsna", literally means "Black", an important Hindu god, an incarnation of Vishnu, second god of the Hindu trinity.

What's interesting about that definition is the fact that Hinduism as the West calls it predates Christianity, yet the concept of a Black Christ already existed as well as the trinity. Krishna literally means Black, and he represents the second part of the trinity, which would be the son in Christianity or Jesus. Notice the name Krishna and Christ is the same word. Then notice all the legitimacy in this word lose its power by placing the g in god as a lower case, to denote a lesser god.

Now let's look up the word "god" in the dictionary. God, which is lower case in

Webster's dictionary, is defined as: M.E. < O.E. akin to German "gott", Goth guth, < IE base "ghau", to call out, invoke. 1. any of various beings conceived of as supernatural, immortal, and having special powers over the lives and affairs of people and the course of nature; deity, esp. a male deity; typically considered objects of worship.

So any cultures "god" can be see as just as important or powerful as the Christian "God", according to the definition of the word. The word "god" also shows the word as a title not an actually personal name, even though the Bible and Christianity give this title a capital letter. This is spell casting done to create an image of power and importance or superiority by simply putting a capital letter on a name. If you look at various Bible characters in the dictionary you will not see the word myth anywhere in the definition as you would if you looked up a character in another mythology. The spell casters in the dictionary placed the word **Bible** in italics and gave a biblical definition of the character according to the Bible when defining it. No doubt words such as myth, folklore, tale, legend are used. Please analyze this! Look up the characters in the Bible and then look up other characters in other mythology and see for yourself. The dictionary is part of a system which cast spells on us by defining words and subliminally endorsing Christianity and its characters as historical and making every other culture's religion or spiritual system mythology, folklore, legends or tales.

Music As A Spell

Music is one of the most powerful mediums to cast spells influencing thinking and behavior. In the 1960's and 70's, the main theme of the musical content was love. Go back and listen to those songs yourself and see everybody was talking about love in their own unique way. This love theme was all in the music, the lyrics and as a result this theme dominated the minds of our people during that time. Even White artist sung about love and anti violence at that time. Love was in the air then and the vibration of the music as a whole had a healing effect on all conscious people. This love energy, through the introduction of new laws, drugs, and economic slavery, turned the tide of love energy and its dominance into a more self centered, egotistical love message by the 1980's. The love theme was there but it was slowly being phased out by the powers that be through the introduction of a new form of music called rap. This music in all reality had no central love theme and R&B was transformed to a more edgy vibration to match the raw street energy of rap. But what created the climate for this musical expression was poverty, drugs and despair, which bred an atmosphere of hopelessness, fear, indecision, and anger. Love music cannot thrive or exist in this condition for long, although we needed this message more than ever. It would be drowned out by the current social and political climate of the times. People began to relate more to the anger and frustration than to the peace and love because of the times they were in. A spell was cast on the music because once the vibration changed after the 1970's; by the time we entered the 80's, new drugs such as crack cocaine entered our community turning people into literal zombies roaming the streets. The love theme was on the peripheral and was replaced by selfish sexuality in R&B, misogynous themes, pimp themes, Black on Black violence and overt drug and alcohol use. Music is a spell because according to the definition of the word **"chant"**, is a song, melody, or statement said in a sing song mode of speaking in which repetition is the key. That's the beat and the lyrics in music! The music sets the atmosphere or is the vehicle and the lyrics or words spoken (rap) or sung (R&B) which are repeated over and over again cast the spell. Think about the lyrics that have come across the radio waves over the last 20 years. The good thing about the computer is that in today's time you can go back and revisit the music of the 60's and 70's for yourself and feel the energy and vibe of this music if you can.   We've been under the spell for so long, I hope the music that the younger generations have been listening to did not destroy their ability to interface with the classic songs of that time! These radio program directors are spell casters and gate keepers of the spell, working to place our minds in a suggestive, hypnotic state, conducive to us being in the mode of irrational emotionality, consumerism, enslavement and self destruction! There's a lot of money to be made in placing people under hypnotic spells. Rap music in general has been used as a major social engineering tool to encourage drug use, drug trafficking, alcohol abuse; abuse of women, Black on Black violence, incarcerations, illegal activity, sexual deviant behavior, mindless consumerism, and the list can go on. It is no coincident that Forbes lists of the most financially successful Hip Hop artist of all time were former drug dealers. The message is loud and clear to anyone willing to listen. These corporations will endorse a former crack dealer to sell their products because in their minds, if you can sell drugs and are willing to destroy your community for financial gain, you're the guy their looking for! You will be willing to sell the people illusions as well as being a puppet for their social engineering. Because these rappers have no morals or ethics like these corporate heads, they are willing participants of our destruction through their music. There's no moral or ethical guidelines that exist which would tell these corporate executives that they shouldn't be endorsing former drug dealers because of the message this endorsement gives. These drug dealers to the industry or power structure are seen only as cash cows that make these men exceedingly rich. These "former" drug dealers are able to manipulate the minds of the youth in order to lead them to a "me first" materialistic lifestyle and attitude that benefits the corporation's bottom line, which of course is money. These youths are given a "blueprint" to success from artist they admire and idolize because these artists have been allowed to become multi millionaires by the corporate and political power structures. Why? To instill a message of self-centeredness, lawlessness, self destruction, materialism designed to destroy the mentality of an African centered consciousness and nationhood in the minds of our people today and of our future generations. African consciousness is extremely vital in the midst of racial constructs. African consciousness is the only real solution for our people and humanity on a whole! This mentality of our unity has been replaced with a "get yours" or "I'm doing me" or "I'm trying to be the next..." mentality, that the true struggle for

African liberation is all but lost! These "artist" have traded their souls for riches and have led a whole generation and generations to come down this destructive self serving path, with no regard for dealing with the true battle we face in 2010 and beyond. That battle being institutionalized racism, racial constructs, genocidal agendas, and historical misrepresentations. None of these multi millionaires are addressing these issues! The neighborhoods they came from looks the same as when they left. This is proof positive that they are puppets for social engineers and spell casters. They have been given wealth, which is a form of power, yet they have no plans on using that wealth to empower their community or address key issues we face head on. They only use their "wealth" to hypnotize you into buying into their self image illusion. If you believe for one moment that these artist "talents" are the reason for all their economic success or their "hard work", you are a fool! People are placed into positions of power very strategically, and this has absolutely nothing to do with talent per se. There are millions of "talented" people in this world, especially in the Black community, yet only a very small amount reaches the status of multi-millionaire. There has to be an approval with the racist power structure at that level, in order to break into all the money markets you see these artists in today. The money itself is not the issue, but how it was obtained and what it is being used for is called into question. The list of rappers telling young people through their example that it is alright to sell drugs, destroy your community, pimp women, and kill to get that money is too long to list. It is these messages that confuse young minds and cast social spells. Think about it; how convenient this "star" becomes a big success after telling the whole world he was a criminal! What a backward message to send to our children? This "star" is overtly and subliminally suggesting a life of crime to our youths as a means to make it out of the hood like them. Just be sure to give back to the community you help destroy by giving them a basketball tournament, some free sneakers, free food on holiday's and of course your music. Come on! You can't see that trap a mile away! You can't see how these rappers and the corporations that support them are contributing to a form of genocide. How do people sell their souls and sell out their people? They do this by helping the beast promote its goals, ideas, and agendas for money and fame in return, whether they know it or not. For example, if I accept a deal (key word) to promote a deadly substance like Malt liquor, which is proven to be hazardous to one's health and known to destroy people's lives, then I just signed over to the "devil". It is that simple. You sold your soul for fame and money. Point blank. You are now a pawn of the "devil". You can never speak out on the ills of Malt liquor, because the deal you made also included your silence on its effects. You can never speak on what you know to be right because this will affect your bottom line, which is money. I purposefully did not mention anyone's name because for one, we all know who they are anyway, it is no secret. Another reason is because I'm not in the business of attacking individuals, but the concept these individuals promote. I think it would be unfair to name some and not all, so I leave you the reader with that responsibility. This is not a complete indictment on rap as a whole either; because I was there when rap commercially first began, and like a lot of us today I honor and respect the art form in its purest form ; however we can see that this art form has been perverted and manipulated from what it was becoming. The negative effects this music has on our people's minds are evident. I must tell the truth about this music whether it hurts people's feelings or not, because our children's lives are at stake! When rappers tried to speak out on the truth or our culture in the 90's it was later suppressed by "gangsta rap". We all went from wearing Black medallions, gaining knowledge of self, a love and respect for ourselves, our history, and our community-- to self destruction seemingly overnight! We went from our brothers and sisters in the West Coast rapping about "we're all in the same gang" and their East Coast brothers and sisters saying "you're heading for self destruction" to it becoming a reality in the big East Coast vs. West Coast rap wars, instigated by rap magazines and other media outlets. Notice those rappers involved in those unity projects can not sell records anymore in high volumes and they are still more skilled than any artist out there! Time will surely tell.

Nigger Mentality As A Spell

It is the mistrust breed in us through the making of a slave and the nigger mentality, which is a hybrid mental state, set in place to ensure our self destruction and servitude to this system. The nigger mentality is another spell cast on our minds through the breaking down of our minds during enslavement. Tribalism and other divisions among us were the seed planted within our culture prior to colonialism, which allowed the nigger mentality to flourish when faced with scientific oppression. Today, this mentality exists as the new plantation is the corporations, which hire these overseers or gate keepers within our race as supervisors to keep the slaves (workers) in line and do their bidding. It's the same mentality being perpetuated for centuries with the same results. Around 1991, I came up with the T-shirt concept called "The Nigga Must Die!" and subsequently I along with members from Third Eye Productions like Mr. Holipsism and Little Mark sold this T-shirt to our community, not to be disrespectful or vulgar, but to send a very strong message about exposing the real villain in our community, which was and is the nigger mentality! This was the simplest yet profound T-shirt I've ever seen. Mr. Holip came up with a T-shirt called "The Bitch Must Die!" to address that mentality that affected our sisters. But both concepts equally apply to both males and females within our community. We sold these T-shirts primarily in Harlem and Brooklyn and since then I have seen the nigger mentality blossom into a giant monster within the Hip Hop culture since we came out against this mentality. People who were "conscious" turned cold hearted and rhymed with venom and hate in their heart as they "spit" this venom on our people and our children. I've witnessed the events that led up to the L.A. riots and all those negative albums that came out before and after that made a big impact on our people's mind. We tried to warn our people in the early 90's about the nigger mentality in our own creative way but most of us in a position to affect the children's minds ran to exploit this mentality for a profit! A big profit! My generation of leaders to come sold us the nigger mentality as the thug era and hustler's era really took off within our music. It hurt me to my heart to see that no lasting solutions were ever put into place by our ancestors to be followed by generation after generation, except this nigger mentality. The nigger mentality keeps us disunited, causes self hate which manifests in Black on Black violence, and keeps us in the role of gatekeeper within the current socio-economic structure. The nigger mentality has to be addressed in terms of keeping us ignorant and stuck in the rut of addictions, self fulfilling prophecies of stagnation and mental death. It is deep family!

Thank the ancestors for the United African Movement back in the 90's for allowing us to combat this nigger mentality by opening up a venue for our people to come and learn about our culture by all the premier Afrikan scholars of that time. Every Wednesday in Brooklyn, New York we would go to a renovated movie theater called The Slave Theatre where our Afrikan consciousness could be cultivated and nourished. Big up to Attorney Alton Maddox and those brothers and sisters behind the scenes that allowed that venue to take place! We heard every Afrikan scholar in our community address this nigger mentality and the solution to it in their own unique way and within the field of their expertise. When the Slave Theater closed down it left a huge void within the movement. Hip Hop changed exponentially after that in my opinion. Even in Harlem, where the Third Eye Production headquarters was located changed. Remember going to Harlem in the early 90's with all the street vendors selling Afrikan conscious books, art, lectures, food, etc.? There was a different energy in the atmosphere and we were on our way to truly waking up before this was removed. This was the beginning of the cure for the nigger mentality, and if left alone would have definitely affected our musical content and our entire culture in a progressive manner. The only thing missing that was sure to eventually come was all of the individual movements uniting and sitting at the table to iron out our differences. Third Eye Productions tried to help facilitate this in that time by interviewing every member of each of the powerful religious or spiritual groups and offering an opportunity to sit at the table to discuss our differences and how we can unify. I interviewed Conrad Muhammad, who at the time was the Minister of Mosque Number 7 from the Nation of Islam. I interviewed members from the Hebrew Israelites located in Harlem, an elder from the Five Percent Nation of God and Earths, and an Imam from the Ansaaru Allah Community out of Philadelphia. In each interview the final suggestion was that they come together to discuss their unification since they all believed in a common enemy destroying our community. We were on our way to making that happen but unfortunately unseen forces and that old nigger mentality blocked this attempt. I still have the video from this and at some point will put it out to show you our involvement in our liberation since we were young. This was prior to youtube, facebook, twitter, blogtalk and all these other computer outlets we use today to disseminate information. It is now in today's time with the advent of these computer networking outlets that we can bring the Slave Theater directly into the homes of our people. There are a lot of brothers and sisters that were there during the early 90's and some are continuing to put out Afrikan conscious information on the internet, on the streets, in lectures, and in books. I salute you all and stand by you. I will NOT allow our differences of opinions to alter our friendships and respect for one another in the name of personal glory or self promotion. We are all family and in this liberation struggle together, forever! I can elaborate extensively on various expressions and aspects of the nigger mentality and will do so in a future work but that is beyond the scope of this book. I will conclude by saying we must confront this mentality first within ourselves as we have all been infected by it, before we can truly deal with it on a national and global level. The Nigga within us MUST DIE!!!

What Is Hindering And/Or Preventing Us From Reaching Our Highest Potential?

What Is Hindering and/or Preventing us from reaching our highest potential, spiritually, mentally, and physically?

Answer: **Fear** and **doubt** are among the top reasons along with a **lack of knowledge of self** and the world around us. **Programmed limitations** and the acceptance of those limits as our reality are other reasons. **White supremacy** or **racism** and racial constructs erected in our lives as inducing feelings **of inadequacy, inferiority complexes**, **self-hate**, **self sabotage**, and **self doubt**. What is hindering us also is scientific technology which includes but is not limited to **mind control techniques**, **mood altering**

techniques, **frequency and vibration manipulation**, **electronic bombardment**, **methane gas bombardment**, **genetically engineered foods** and various other distraction techniques to name a few.

Western scientists claim we only use less than 10% of our brain power. I do not know how they truly determine this or measure this, but the fact that their saying this is quite revealing. If we are only using less than 10% of our mind's potential, what is keeping us from accessing more? Our divine mental potential is being purposefully hindered by a racist power structure in this world called global White supremacy. Its very existence acts as an inhibitor to natural genius and our ability to reach higher levels of mental and spiritual access. Racism attempts to rob us of our ability to achieve our maximum potential because of the chronic stress caused by the constant and consistent attack on our psyche and physical body. The body is overworked at these jobs or plantations, whether it includes standing up all day, moving around all day, on the computer all day, or attempting to solve their problems all day. Fatigue and exhaustion is a primary element that induces stress both mentally and physically. Once stress reaches its optimum level, the immune system is compromised, thus the body is now susceptible to sickness or dis-eases. We are a tired people! We are all stressed out! We are tired of the condition we are in, have been in and want a major change NOW!! In old time slavery, our ancestors worked from sun up to sun gone, working vigorously in this country under the constant conditions of fear and stress. The fear of the whip or fear of death, or fear of losing a loved one who might get sold away, or fear of being sold to another slave "master" because they didn't perform up to the standards of a lazy ass slave owner. Sounds familiar? In today's time it is the modern day plantation called the corporation that illicit those same fears. We are overworked having to give now 80 hours of labor before we receive compensation or money. Also, we are using all of our mental and physical stamina and energy for their jobs all under the threat of being terminated which in today's economy is equivalent to a financial death! This death will cause major losses such as your home or apartment, your car, your children (when you can not pay child support you will lose custody), your freedom (if your on probation and your not working, you violated a condition of your release thus will be sent to jail), etc. You see how all this is a modern day slavery. Of course you do! The only thing that makes some of you feel different about your slavery or actually enjoy it is that when you go home you have more freedoms to entertain yourself in between slaving for these jobs. Big deal! So what if you can go to the liquor store after work, or buy some drugs to keep you numb to your present reality or watch television or play your video games all night or go to some social club or event. All that was given to you or allowed to appease you to make you accept this modern day enslavement without a major revolt among the people, that's all. We do not spend our "free" time plotting and planning our escapes from this enslavement. No, we'd rather relax enough to serve our masters for another 80 hours before we receive compensation for our labor. This new slavery applies to Whites as well. Yes they're in slavery as well. The main difference in their bondage and others is that they have much more privileges on the plantation/ job and less stress overall than we have. Look around you and notice how more relaxed Whites are on your job than Blacks. If you and your friends are caught taking a break or talking on some of these plantations, the gatekeepers have something to say? If Whites are talking or taking a break, usually nothing is said, and if something is said it is either due to our provocation or after a long period of time. Count the amount of whites fired versus the amount of other races at your job. Don't take my word for it; check this out for yourself. Why? Because this system inherently protects them over us and this is why you can not find White freedom fighters because they want the system to stay the way it is. So we get stuck at these dead end jobs, which stands for Just Over Broke for years and years because we are so mentally and physically exhausted after giving so much of our life force for their benefit that most of us do not have the energy nor discipline to work toward that which matters most after work.   We go into shut down mode and seek out escapes. It is very understandable just not beneficial. Please do not think you're benefiting from that little bit of money you get to make them billions of dollars.   You do not receive anywhere near the compensation you deserve from the corporations you serve. This is all by design to keep us stuck and used as a battery for their system.   Our potential is limitless mentally and spiritually, and even our physical potential have yet to become fully realized due to constraints that have been placed in our minds as a result of racism. We are stuck because we don't have financial institutions or corporations that hire and service our people exclusively the way the Jews have or the Chinese have in their community. They are allowed to hire their own and work exclusively for their nations benefit throughout this county yet nothing is said to be wrong with their exclusion. When was the last time you went to any China town USA and saw a black owned business? When was the last time you saw an Afrikan working at a Chinese restaurant or hair and nails salon? When was the last time you went into a Jewish community and saw a black business there? Do they hire blacks or Latinos in their community? Is this an unfair observation or the truth? Why is that not seen as racism or a problem? Why don't we adopt the same mentality and trade with the world but financially empower only our people like they do? This applies to the Arabs as well. These groups mentioned take the dollars made by us and take it out of our community to build their own. Why can't we do the same? When are we going to take back our own products and starve them out like they do us? When are we going to set up businesses in their community and sell them their products like they do us?

Also our untapped spiritual power hinders our development. We are not practicing our traditional spiritual systems in the modern era. We have been taught to discredit them and be afraid of them. Thus our powers to change our conditions are dormant, untapped, redirected, and misused. We must return to our traditional spiritual systems and its knowledge to awaken the deity within us. Western religions will not do this for us because it hasn't yet. We are afraid to call on our ancestors because Western religion has labeled this devil worship or the practice of divination or speaking to our ancestors as evil! Their so called holy books even speak out against our traditional systems. We don't eat in a holistic way to access the divine through natural foods and herbs. Western religion has taught us that it doesn't matter what you eat as long as you pray over your food in the name of Jesus. So we won't drink herbal teas and eat of the foods that directly interface with our bodies and consciousness in ways that will transform us. We don't analyze our dreams anymore to gain insight, information and as a vehicle to communicate with our ancestors. We don't see the dream world as real and relevant to our journey in the "waking world", so we are cut off from its message. We don't meditate properly, but use prayer methods dictated by religions taught by our oppressors that keep us enslaved and asleep. We don't know which deity to call on or which aspect of the one creator is responsible for the particular area in our lives that need addressing. We don't serve our "God" and the deities responsible for our lives but rather serve our oppressors god and their ancestors. All of these things mentioned are hindering and preventing us from reaching our highest potential and stagnating our progress as individuals and collectively. Our souls are trapped in a foreign body and within an alien mind state! We must relearn everything we have been taught and made to believe about ourselves, our history and reality itself. It is only then that we will unlock the chains and shackles that keep us dormant, under control and locked down. We have lost our intuitive knowledge and replaced them for a faulty belief system called religion. We must get free of these things and return back home mentally and spiritually first so the physical body can follow. Ase!

Who Perpetrates, Creates And Enforces This Spell?

The media is a major contributor to the spell and this includes **all** major newspapers, television companies, radio companies, and movie producers. They have a unified agenda and actually meet annually or periodically to discuss their agenda and compare notes with one another. That's why if you look at a particular issue or world event, all these media outlets are more or less saying the same thing. They're all on the same page with the overall theme, message, or point of view they want us to focus on or believe in. Check it out for yourself. Think about September 11th and do a search on how all the newspapers in this country covered that story from the beginning. The media shapes public opinion and programs people into accepting what is actual news worthy material and to accept staged realities, along with enforcing stereotypes of the Black male and female image across the world. Government creates laws that enforce racial biases and superiority of Whites as has been the case since the foundation of this country, to the Emancipation Proclamation, to Jim Crow laws and segregation to today's legal landscape. The law always works in favor of Whites across this globe and this is obviously by design to keep them the ruling class of minority among the majority of non White world citizens. White people are actually the overwhelming minority in this world and even in America, yet they cast the spell of words on us by saying we are the minority thus creating the perception which becomes the reality.

Religious leaders perpetuate and enforce this spell by keeping our people locked into an oppressive mythology and inaccurate worldview. These "leaders" are actually gatekeepers and overseers designed to subvert our Afrikan consciousness and keep us asleep. They are working whether consciously or unconsciously against our ancestors and the unification of our Afrikan spirit. They must be challenged and their false concepts exposed as the lies they are. Spiritual pimps are what I call them and they are allowed to become financially successful in this "devil's" world because they serve the "devil's" agenda. They are not speaking the truth and this can, and will be revealed in due time.

Our family and friends perpetrates and enforces this spell as well. It was from the mouth of those we trust and love that gave us the white supremacist mythology called

Christianity and endorsed it. I love them and honor them still because they were ignorant of our history and the facts but corrections must be made. This is our duty in this generation. We will not hate or fight our elders that fell victim to the spell, but we will not allow our children to become victims either. We cannot afford to lose another generation! Family is not just those born in your house. Some family members are placed in your genealogy to stop you from self realization or to challenge your stance on your culture. Take the time to enlighten them if you chose but do not get caught up in endless debates with them either. Show and prove by your example rather than your words. Do not let them become a stumbling block for you, but continue to show them the love and patience they deserve. Our friends also act as gatekeepers and conscious ceilings which keep us stagnated or reaching the next level. It's okay to make new alliances and friends. Those old friends are keeping us in that old paradigm we were in when we met them. Again we love them, but it's time to get free and if they are not with that or not ready to embrace that, then its time to respectfully move on. We cannot allow old friends to keep us in an old mind state. Either they elevate or we remove ourselves from their influence for the sake of the big picture. Don't be egotistical about it, but rather show humility and stand firm on your stance. If you argue with a fool, from a distance it's hard to tell who is who! Remember that always.

Where Exactly Is This Hypnotic Spell Taking Us?

Back down the evolutionary scale to some primordial man or pre "our story" man. If you look at the way this spell has our people acting and looking, you will see a genetic regression that resembles a dark age for our people. The spell is designed to completely wipe out our genetic memory of our glorious past, thus ensuring we will never attain our glorious future and regain our role as models in world citizenship, intellect and spirituality to everyone on this planet. Our role has been supplanted by the White race in an aggressive take over to deceive the world, and for the most part his plans have been successful. Just like the story of Jacob in the bible deceiving his father in a plot to steal his brother's birthright and supplant him! However falsehood cannot last because it was not built on truth and righteousness and this is stated in nearly every religion across this planet and within history. Evil cannot ultimately defeat good. His rule on the planet earth has been horrible. Look at the status of the planet earth and judge for yourself. Any group of people that knowingly destroys our planet in the name of capitalism is not fit to rule or be in a position of leadership. So anti life and synthetic that it appears "the powers that be" feel alienated from nature and are rogue world citizens. A lot of our people have assumed this same vibe of being denatured through the spell. This spell is also destroying our sense of personal responsibility to the things occurring on our planet, in our countries and within our communities. While under this hypnotic trance we have been programmed to think that we must wait for those "in charge" or appointed as leaders to fix our current conditions, while we sit back and complain or feel powerless to involve ourselves in the long process of rebuilding. Human beings are really being further isolated from each other to create an individualistic society which can be controlled through personal greed, and thus allow the synthetic interface with the computer. The cyborg or half man half computer/machine is the direction these planetary leaders are going to use to control the populace and act as a buffer between them and ordinary citizens that logically will rebel against this form of control to come. The computer is the gift and the curse. This invention has made aspects of our lives easier yet there is a hidden danger in its presence as well. Remember before the cell phone was put on the market, we had to memorize or use our minds to recall our family and friends number? Well now the cell phone has erased that capacity because no one has any numbers memorized anymore! We find the person's name and press a button to call them. We have systematically lost aspects of our brain power and gave it over to the computer! Technology has interfaced with our experience so deeply that we find it hard to think and exist without it. We are being taken over by the computer and giving birth to everything we see in the movies in terms of the eventual conquest of humans by the machine! When will we realize this plot? Discussions in schools today are centered on "Can machines think?" and what is the difference between a computer and the human brain? So this spell is taking us into a new matrix of enslavement that involves this computer and modern day technology. We are so dependent on this technology that to live without it will soon be impossible if we are not there already! I think the latter is true. We have to periodically unplug from the computer and exist without it to hear clear the message of our divine selves. The information we need to be really in tune with is not found on the internet or a computer screen. This information is to be found within. If we don't do this I'm telling you our next slave master will be the computer, technology and the cyborg machine man/woman! This is real and it's happening as we speak. We are heading for that reality right now! Remember the scene in the Matrix when Neo woke up and found himself plugged into a computer generated dream world being fed an artificial reality or intelligence? Don't be deceived or naïve family because this is happening now!

Understanding The Spell Of Distractions

Observe the energy surrounding you as you enter and leave buildings. Notice what is said around you or any loud abrupt behavior or words. Do not become distracted by these things, just become aware of them as distractive elements nor get caught up emotionally in any of it. The real purpose of the spirit of distractions or the energy around distractions is to cause you to not pay attention to what you should be doing, was doing or want to do. This spell of distraction is caused primarily by energy vampires seeking to draw your focus or energy into their chaos and confusion. This is not always the case of course as some distractions can be life saving and beneficial. You should be able to tell the difference between a beneficial distraction and one that entails nonsense meaningless confusion. Another distraction is when someone calls out to another person using a generic term, instead of their name such as "hey you!" or "excuse me!" "Yo!" and "hello!" These are all distractions, since no personal names are involved it tends to draw a spirit of confusion in everyone around this utterance, because no one knows who is being spoken to yet everyone feels obligated to react. This might not be done with intent to be manipulative or confusing by the person saying this of course, but it is distractive and does bring about a spirit of confusion in that moment nevertheless. Observe people's reaction when this is done and you can see what I'm talking about. Therefore, the main objective of distraction is to derail or suspend your focus or thought ranging from partially to totally. If you notice people involved in illegal activity use this tactic, as well as in the prisons. Old time con men and hoodlums used this as a decoy to fool their victims into placing themselves in harm's way or as a way to make a person show their hand or reveal their true emotional state which probably was fear or confusion. **Is a self distraction pattern created once you lose even slight control of your emotions? How about when you unconsciously lead yourself to become distracted** or increase the possibility **to be distracted? Why do you think you were compelled to further your possibilities of becoming distracted?** A moment of applied force used to change your focus can and will alter the outcome of events if only your emotional state of being is even slightly pulled out of control, you will become distracted a percentage. It might only be unnoticeably small but nevertheless it will be a slight distraction.

This theory is observed through years of personal case study. Something else I have observed over the years is what I call "**The Downward Spiral Effect of Negativity.**" This is defined loosely as a negative downward spiral of energy that occurs after an initial negative emotion, reaction, action, or thought. This is somewhat similar to the self fulfilling prophecy theory in that what you continue to dwell on can become fulfilled through your own thought power. Or where your mind and intent shifts toward the idea you are placing your energy on creates the possibilities of that idea to manifest whether positive or negative. Because most of the energy around us is already negative could be the key reason negative energy has more momentum to continue down the spiral and into fulfillment faster than positive energy. So we wonder why we can not get more money or have more positive experiences in life, or why when we think of something good that we want to happen in our lives it seems to take much longer to happen than something negative. You need twice the energy to create a positive result because of the **Downward Spiral Effect of Negativity**. That's why it is very important to maintain a calm positive mental attitude about things. Once your mental state becomes entangled in all the negative vibrations surrounding you, with all the fear, worry and anger in the atmosphere from this global oppression; any negative thought generated within your own mind or intent can travel down the spiral and into a negative outcome because of the momentum it has already accumulated.

Another distraction method people use is to watch you perform or use their eyes as a magnet to draw you into their mind state or current emotional state. With the energy that exists in vision they are forcefully attempting to pull you into their drama using the power of staring. You may find yourself being observed unannounced or uninvited by staring eyes and actually feel energy being sucked from you. Of course you can not stop someone from looking at you but you can remove their energy or block the energy they're absorbing by taking the focus off them and using their energy to benefit yourself. This is why you see a lot of celebrities wearing shades when they're out in the public "eye". They're trying to control and block the energy that is coming toward them from being in the midst of all that energy coming from people staring at them all the time. Can you imagine all the energy these high profile celebrities absorb from people on a daily basis? I guess that's the price of fame right? They wear sunglasses or shades to protect their energy from energy vampires. This shows you the power emitting from the eyes and how it can both cast spells and manipulate energy. This is what the "evil eye" is all about. If someone is on stage performing that's one thing .The presence of all that energy from staring is expected and mentally accounted for, but even that has huge distractive elements. Can you imagine how unnerving it could be to be stared at by large groups of people all day? The best actors performing live on stage are the ones that are so mentally involved in their role that they block out even the existence of an audience. A great actor has a very powerfully developed mental ability to avoid distractions as does a great athlete. These people, within their profession, have trained themselves to master distractions coming from thousands and millions of different energies all with various intents. When people watch you do something without your permission or desire, it creates an uncomfortable feeling or vibe and can throw you off focus or make you become hyper aware of what you're doing and place you in the role of performer for the people watching. You can lose your center or focus by becoming their center of attention! Supervisors in the work place do that a lot, creating a feeling of fear and confusion, if you let them.

Notice what you're thinking about or doing when someone asks you for directions. Notice a loud noise occurs or a major distraction when you are speaking on something significant or about to have a conscious breakthrough. White people are notorious for distracting or interrupting Blacks when they are in a discussion on something important, meaningful or deep. If you think this is an unfair indictment, then observe this in your life from now on and you will see, especially at work! When the conversation centers around sports, television programs and other junk, the distractions aren't there; however as soon as the talk is on current events, Black advancement, racism, or spiritual development, you can hardly finish your sentence before someone walks into the conversation to pull you off that energy. Notice I said pull you off, not interrupt the conversation to add something meaningful to it, but to derail that thought or intercept that breakthrough. I know a lot of you know exactly what I'm talking about. If there isn't something deep in that, explain why this always occurs?

What is the significance of 5pm, 7pm and 9pm? Observe what's going on around you and within you during these times. As a matter of fact, set your alarm to these times as a test and record the results. Observe how lights play a role in your conscious state. Notice how you feel or think in the dark, in a dimly lit room, and when the sun goes down. Also notice how you think and feel in a well lit or over lit environment. People who are always talking about others rather than insights, useful information or something positive, if you study their characteristics are: bitter, angry, revengeful, spiteful, and negative. These are the same individuals on their jobs that have been there forever or will be there forever and have no plans of doing anything else with their lives. They are the gate keepers of the slave mentality. These people gossip, start rumors, get people fired, get flu shots at work, and overall, maintain the Negro mentality through everything they do and say. Observe them and see for yourself if you're not one of them! If you are one of these people, look deeply into yourself and change your attitude and mentality through knowledge of self and sincerity.

Why are Black people so afraid to speak on and fight for our liberation in this global oppression? Study the game of chess and attempt to master this game. We need to see Black grandmaster chess players. There's a lot you can learn from learning the game of chess, which originally is a Black invention anyway. If you already play chess continue to perfect your game.

Study movies as propaganda and learn to see the hidden truths and omissions in these movies. When or if you attend the movies, bring a small pad with you to jot down any ideas or breakthroughs you may have. Do not go to the movies, but to breakdown the meaning of the subject or any themes which will help you uncover a greater or hidden truth. Do some research into the subject or topic of the movie prior to you going so you can clearly see the omissions and the deception? This is especially true for historical movies or movies based on some historical event. Notice the characters and the dialogue. Do they represent the image this historical character represented in real life? Did they omit key events within the story? Why? What did they put in its place? Pay attention to how the dialogue is spoken and what is said and not said. A lot of times the movies have a habit of quickly addressing key statements or issues or transitioning from major statements to silly or irrelevant ones in order to undermine or trivialize the meaning or implication of those statements. Attention span is the key. Once we breakdown our thinking process and how our body is reacting to this spell, we can then reverse the effects of century old programs instilled in us and delete those outdated files of lies and misinformation and return to become normal, healthy, productive world citizens again. We will return back to our true and original Self.

Spell of Manipulation

We must study the science of unlearning everything we've been programmed to know, believe and accept as real.

In our look at manipulation, let's look at person to person manipulation. Here are a few questions to ponder pertaining to this subject:

1. What constant theme is present in a manipulative situation?
2. Define clearly what the principles of manipulation are?
3. When are we most likely, least likely, or never likely to be manipulated? Why not?
4. Define Positive Manipulation.
5. What are the various levels of manipulation?

Goals of Manipulation

1. To gain energy control whether positive or negative.
2. To gain advantage in motion.
3. To cause change in thought whether positive or negative.
4. To cause change in motion.
5. To cause change in perception
6. Gain/causation/control study

Manipulation works when an applied force is used to coerce the victim into a particular thought, word or action of manipulation which best meets the objective of the manipulator. The common denominator of manipulation is Intent/content divided by Control/results. The pattern of manipulation begins within the psyche of the individual, who perceives it necessary to manipulate others to achieve a goal or objective that they feel they cannot accomplish on their own, or not without the aid of someone else. The conversion of energy depends on manipulating the victim into another direction or a desired direction. How is this accomplished? First, the reaction knowledge of the subject or what information motivates them to respond or show emotions, which is energy in motion, is determined.

Second, the link point or the point where the victim is linked through the universal affinity point to fulfill the needs of others or self is determined. The manipulator can come sincere and emotional, like Hollywood does in its movies, and thus deepens the link point of compulsion toward action on the part of the manipulated. This is when they take a character and show them playing with children or displaying some characteristic you relate to as positive or good. Now you are rooting for the character or sympathizing with the character at that point. So if the character does something evil or contradictory, you have already developed a justification for their actions based on past scene emotional ties. This is how you can relate to historical characters that were anti Afrikan in real life but still cry for their character and feel sorry for them within the movie. It is both ingenious and powerfully manipulative. Depending on the intensity of the link point of love or desire between the manipulator or its object and the subject will depend on the degree to which manipulation will work, never work, or always work. The stronger the emotional ties are, the deeper the link point toward action or reaction and the more likely the manipulation will be a success. Even if the manipulator is a complete stranger, he/she can still produce a manipulative effect if the content of their manipulative drama or object is high enough on the emotional scale for the one manipulated.

The real purpose of distraction is to take your mind or perception off the real or what the illusion is, or intended target of focus and onto another point designed to divert your attention. So the question to be asked is, if left undistracted at the moment of distraction, what would you be doing, thinking, or saying? This whole illusion of distraction and manipulation is to again, distract you from perceiving, exposing or reflecting on the "real" within the illusion, which is labeled the distraction. Distractions most people use on a daily basis are used to receive attention or energy from someone else, which is mostly negative. **Keeping people distracted is one of**

the major pillars of the Spell. What happens to a thought when it is distracted? Thoughts derail or go off track when an incident takes place within your field or range of awareness that removes you from the path of thought you were on. This is how people who start out positive can turn negative. In mathematics, how does a positive turn into a negative? The answer is fixed in multiplication as a set principle. Meaning positive times a positive will always be positive and negative times a positive will always be negative! In adding or subtracting positive and negative numbers, the larger number carries the sign. This principle is the key to understanding distractions from a mathematical perspective. If you are bombarded with negativity, your outcome or the results will unfortunately be negative. That's the key reason why such a concentrated effort is made to keep the news negative, the talk shows negative, the movies negative, the music negative, and the television negative. All these negatives will turn into a negative for you as well, because this is a mathematic principle. Now do you see the dangers of watching all that negativity on the television, in the movies, and on the radio? This is proof that these negatives *will* and does affect our state of mind and bring us into negativity. The answer is stop watching these things. No one told you that you have to watch the news everyday when you wake up and before you go to bed. Do you see how you are being put under a spell first thing in the morning and the last thing before you go to bed? Then you wonder why your day turned out negative or why you have to use an escape drug to cope. You may also wonder why your dreams are so negative and unproductive in terms of getting information to be used in the "waking world." Its because of all the fear and death on the news you saw right before bed!

In reality all our emotions which vary from person to person, are under constant and consistent assault every waking second we exist. That's why people abuse and misuse drugs, violence, sex, or alcohol. We are unconsciously emotional reactionary robots in this matrix being put into a self destruct program using manipulation and distractions as its main mode of operation! The good news is you can do something about all these negative implants and distractions, but will you? You can unplug from all the sensory stimulation that is causing all the negativity, distractions, manipulations, and emotional roller coasters. You can do this by stop watching television, even if for a while until you gain more self control or knowledge, stop listening to commercial bombardments which program your mind through suggestions and fear, stop mindlessly entertaining yourself with the media and use the media to gain information you can use. And lastly please stop reading misinforming sensationalized newspapers and watching the same kind of news on television and the internet. It is not real news, but propaganda designed to control our thoughts and focus, and have us absorbed in what they deem is news or "THE" topic of discussion. It is all manipulation my family and we really should unplug from it. You will see how different you vibrate when you do as compared to co-workers, friends, or family that is still hooked on television or the news. You will see how clear your thoughts will become and how you will avoid substances naturally as a result of being free from the programs and propaganda. At least become aware of the spell while watching the "program". Start to notice the things said in the commercials and challenge those concepts! Pay attention to the music played during these programs and commercials as well. We all know how powerful music is. Imagine watching a horror movie without the music. It probably wouldn't scare you at all. I suggest you try it and see for yourself. Don't be afraid to experiment with this spell to uncover the power it has on you for yourself! Watch your scariest movie without sound. Be a scientist and see for yourself the things that entrap you. "Messing with someone's head", means manipulating them emotionally to react to some staged dialogue or action in which the person initiating the dialogue is purposefully leading the respondent into an emotional trap. Nurturing or feeding this energy of manipulation is self-destructive. Get the energy to dissipate by ignoring it, and if you can not ignore it totally, then ignore its energy within yourself. Anger like any other negative emotion is a germ, which spreads from one person to the next through personal contact by the mouth (words), the eyes (eye contact), and the body (contact and gestures). A big cause of relationships ending or its failure to start is this phenomenon of energy manipulation and how it is misunderstood. **Miscommunication is to miss out on communicating**. The eyes are symbolic windows to the soul, not the soul itself. The reflection your eyes show reflect your awareness, temperament, and mood at that moment to most people. Only to an individual who has mastered themselves sufficiently enough can see your true self in your eyes. Only the unprejudiced soul can see your true intent and nature through your eyes at any moment. 95% of the population can only see what you show them and only sense something different. One of the things robbed from us is a clear state of mind. Our mentality constantly exists in chaos and confusion, thus are unable to exist in the clarity of the now. We are constantly and systematically being driven into a state called insanity. There is a magnetic attraction toward negativity and Black people have, through trillions of dollars spent, been manipulated mentally by the media, education, entertainment, politics, the law, race propaganda, and historical lies and misrepresentations to remain in a chronic state of negativity. To be prepared for the real spiritual war, you must master all these distractions and manipulations around you and even the one's that are now self inflicted as a result of distractive programming.

Language as a Spell

English is a bastardize language that's comprised of many different languages i.e. French, German, Latin, Greek, etc. English as a language is the master control language worldwide, as it is the power language of today's world. People that speak English have a habit of judging someone's intelligence according to how they use and understand this language. For example, if a Chinese person speaks English, because his language does not have a rolling "r" sound in it, he must modify the English words that have this sound in it. This does not make him less intelligent, he or she is merely adjusting to his culture's language mode. If a person speaking English was to try and learn Chinese, they would soon see how intelligent that Chinese person really is! Same thing with Blacks and the way we might omit word's in the English language formation that is labeled grammatically incorrect. Incorrect for whom I ask? The purpose of language is communication not to get hung up on silly rules of speaking and labeling what's correct and what's not. This is classism through the use of language and a form of language control that's used to keep people spellbound. Also this use of language is a means to identify who is programmed under the English language spell's control paradigm. There are certain concepts pertaining to higher spirituality and vibration that do not exist within the Euro-American English language. Certain intuitive knowledge is lost merely by speaking English! There are other ways to access this information, but it requires a full submission to the meaning and knowledge of hidden language. For example, the word

"God" is a Germanic word not an African, Asian, or Indigenous American word, yet that word as a concept is the most powerful word in the English language. So the most powerful and potent concept is only known to us as a German derivative word and not in our true language! Think about that. When you refer to the ultimate force governing life as you know it by the name "God", you have placed yourself deep into the language spell of European culture and made impotent the name of your "God" in your original languages. Remember words are power, and so our "God" (remember god according to the dictionary is a title not an actual name) remains dormant in our hearts and minds because we have lost contact with that divine name. No wonder we're in this current predicament, we are using the wrong name and language to call on our ancestors and even our Creator! If your name is Malik, but I keep calling you

Steve; after a while you will ignore me, because the name Steve has no meaning or power over you as to respond to it. Think about that. The dictionary is in the business of creating spells through words and it is always adding new words to replace others to create class barriers or as indicators to an individuals intelligence or assimilation to the spell. This explains is the power behind what happened to us when we lost our languages. That had devastating consequences to our ability to become divorced from our entire culture or way of life. The language barrier is as deep as the Grand Canyon and it places our consciousness in a very complicated situation and might be the root of our disunity, confusion, and overall stagnation as a people. We have to return to this artificial language to explain and view reality thus we have become lost.

Clothing as a Spell

What you wear identifies who you are to the world.   Your clothing also identifies your state of mind, religion, gender or sexual orientation, social status and profession. Each culture or race has their own clothing which identifies them as a unique group on the planet earth.   When you remove a people from their cultural dress or clothing, you have made them unidentifiable, and removed their cultural connection and distinction to themselves and the rest of the world.   How would you identify a police officer in our society? You would identify them by their uniform. If they do not have their uniform on, are they still police officers? Yes they are but they are unidentifiable to society dressed in civilian clothing.   They only become officers to us when they have on the clothing that identifies them as such. Now, as African people through colonialism, imperialism, and slavery we have been stripped of our cultural attire. Even those of us that we're already here before Columbus arrived with his "discovery" of the "New World", were taken out of our royal dress. We have been given Western style clothes to wear and most of us feel ashamed to wear our own culture's garb. Even Black owned clothing companies or designers model their clothing after White designers, like Italians for example. Instead of having African based patterns and designs they give us a European style of clothing to wear. Not only does the clothing Afrikans wear today reflect cultural amnesia and colonialism but our women are tricked into wearing their hair in a colonized fashion. Ashamed of our natural beauty and cultural expression, we are quick to adopt another culture's fashion over our own. This is another sad example of media propaganda, miseducation, and self hate at its finest. Look at how the urban youth has adopted a prison style of dress with their pants falling below their butts. In prison, inmates are forbidden to wear belts because a belt can be used as a weapon against the correction officers and other inmates. Also a belt can be used as a tool for suicides. What happened as a result of the no belt policy is the sag of the pants or the pants falling off the butt of the inmate. This played into a number of scenarios that only prison life can create. Unfortunately this pants sagging became for some an erotic invitation and for others a means to display their availability for that invitation. Now fast forward to today's time where "free" young men are copying the style of dress of those incarcerated as a warped fashion statement. These young men and now women are walking around with their underwear showing or their pants nearly at their knees! Clearly this is some form of deep hypnotics at work here and the results of such a dress code only falls in synch with the feminization of the Black man, promotion of homosexuality among today's youth as a normal behavior mode, and the cartoon or buffoon image of the Black man on the world stage. We as responsible Black adults should demand that these young people pull their pants up as any group of people should. According to local police laws all across this country there is a law called "indecent exposure". Interesting that this law is not enforced when it comes to Black men displaying this demeaning dress in front of their own community! If you think this is not done on purpose to mock our community and show the world the state of Blacks and what our future holds, then you are in deep denial.

Drugs as a Spell

The use of substances to alter our reality, mood, experience, or consciousness, has been with us for thousands of years. The thing that needs to be analyzed about all drugs and its use is the reason why we need to use it. The reason drug use is so rampant in the Black community in particular is the current racial construct we live under and are subjected to on a daily basis. This capitalistic vampire system that sucks our blood like brother Bob Marley said, is the reason why we feel we must escape it, even if temporarily. I fully understand why we would chose to press the escape hatch on this downpressive system, and I truly do not judge anyone in the decisions they make. I'm speaking to my family from a strategic point of view on if these substances will serve our best interest in the long term. That's my focus. The "why" we use is my focus and the ramifications of its use. Racism builds up such a tension within the mind, with all the mental gymnastics one must do to hold your head at work or in society to keep from flipping out on someone, that the liquor store or the dealer might seem to be the natural remedy. This racial system understands our minds and reactions very well, since they've had a long time to study us and document their findings. We've also had a very long time to study them as well; it is just that we have only recently documented our findings. Racism knows that a condition must be created to create the environment for drug use. If in optimal condition or in natural conditions without a stressor like racism or capitalism, I can almost guarantee we would not even have the desire to use any drug or substance.

Why would we? That's like being on vacation in a new country and spending the whole time in the hotel getting drunk or high. You wouldn't even be motivated to do that because the environment does not allow that. You want to be out to experience that new environment not stuck in the hotel. The problem to be dealt with is the way we are handling racism. To submerge yourself in a fish tank or dwell in a cloud of smoke, might temporarily relieve some stress but in the end, it will make you an ineffective soldier in the fight for our liberation. Did Harriet Tubman drink or smoke before she gathered our people on their journey out of bondage? Did Malcolm X or Martin Luther King Jr. have to smoke a blunt before they gave their speeches that changed our lives today? Once you place a substance in the position of generator or the engine to make your consciousness function, you are playing a dangerous game with yourself and your people. First of all, the marijuana quality on these urban streets today are substandard poisons, that have been sprayed with roach spray, pesticides, dipped in embalming fluid, etc. all to enhance the trash that it is. Are your children to follow this path to escape? Is your child to choose this example to deal with racism? In order to truly assume leadership and responsibility at home and on the world stage, we have to live our lives sober. You got to be sober to take over. We all have addictions to deal with and confront no matter who you are or who you think you are! Our self honesty and sober group support will allow us to use all of our hidden potential for the betterment of ourselves and our community. I only ask the questions as the decisions you make is of course up to you. But I'll end by saying; the time it takes to get high or drunk could be spent really providing and implementing *real* solutions to our problems, not temporary escapes. Because once you've finished that cocaine, heroin, pill, weed or that drink, racism still exists and your stress is still there. Your issues are still there. But now things are a little more complicated because now you have to factor into the equation your addictions and how to keep getting high to handle all the stress. This will drain your vitality, finances, focus, discipline and set you back again to ground zero. You have to bottom out again to start from scratch every time you choose to use that one time. That is called the **Cycle of Addiction** and it is very real indeed. If you were never sober before, I would strongly suggest you drink herbal teas, bitters, and live fruits and vegetables and get clean. Once you drink these live foods you will begin to lose all desire to drink or smoke. I strongly suggest you become a **Soldier Of Sobriety** and put down the alcohol (except during ceremonial libations if that is not your addiction; if alcohol is your weakness, use water instead), cigarettes (totally), all other drugs of course, and marijuana (it is a trap in the end family). That's why marijuana is called weed, because you become entangled in that weed and get stuck. We do not need to be high on weed to reach spiritual insights, get enlightened or think deep. Once you wrap marijuana up in paper or tobacco and burn it you just changed the element of the herb to a processed food! It becomes a drug at that point that affects your thinking, focus and reality, in ways that are not all positive. I'm sure we will have many that will disagree; however for your children's generation I would say to them to not smoke anything. The only thing hot that should be going into your body that's an herb is herbal tea! If you must smoke herb, it should be done ceremonially and with a pad and pen or recorder to record your insights. If you're not willing to do this then don't smoke in my opinion. Also the frequency in which you smoke must be very limited. To smoke everyday is counterproductive. To smoke mindlessly is also counterproductive. There are some people who do not let the herb master them, but if you are not completely honest with yourself, you can fall victim to becoming addicted to smoking herb and lose any benefits it might offer. You should also purposefully go long periods of time without smoking even if you intend to smoke in the future. The question is when do we age out from smoking? Are we going to be 60 years old still getting high? When is the end? Stay sober and let's win our minds back family, if not for us then for our children; mines and yours. We must become **Soldiers of Sobriety!**

Food As A Spell

You are what you eat! We have been placed under a spell through the foods we've been taught to eat. The average American 3 course meal is in actuality a menu of death and disease! We have been programmed to consume animal flesh, animal fluids (milk), genetically modified organisms, sugar, salts, high fructose corn syrup, pharmaceutical drugs, fast foods, boxed foods, can foods, devitalized foods, candy, cakes, etc. And we wonder why we have chronic illnesses, high infant mortality, morbid obesity, and all these cancers! The foods we eat were NOT our ancestor's choice of foods before slavery. When our people were brought here to these lands to be used as a slave and those of us that were already here before they came, we ate off the land and lived a very healthy, long life. There were no fast food restaurants, package stores or liquor stores, candy shops and grocery stores selling boxed, canned and plastic death! Our ancestors were brought to these lands and left their foods behind. Slave traders did not bring the natural foods and medicines our people lived off of for centuries, when they brought them over as slaves to their country. They came and got our medicines later on when diseases ran rampart, but still tried to prevent us from using our own natural medicines. Fast forward to today's time and they have a drug for every symptom known to man yet no cures. The cure for ALL diseases on this planet can be found in some natural herb or plant. Notice there are no television commercials for natural herbs, but you will find plenty of drug commercials advertised every day. Food is the one thing no one can live without, so the spell to control what you consume as a means to control you is at the top of the list. Look at **Codex Alimentarius** and see what this directive is all about in terms of controlling the food supply on this planet. Why do you think these biotech companies investing in these genetically modified organisms have all your favorite politicians in the palm of their hands? These companies are the new global farmers and what they are doing is monopolizing seeds, which are as natural as air, and genetically modifying them so they cannot be replanted after its season of use has ended. This genetic advance is all courtesy of injecting an herbicide or pesticide gene into the crop in addition to cross breeding animals and crops from totally different species! The results of such tampering with the genetic makeup of foods are said to be currently unknown, highly debated and speculated on yet very obvious if you want to see. Look at your foods in your local supermarkets and you will see 90% of those foods containing wheat, corn or soy derivatives. These are the main three crops that have been genetically altered by the biotech companies. Do the research for yourself! Our favorite president, Mr. Obama, has no intent to stop any of this from happening either. The global food spell is a go and all of our genes are being altered into something totally different than what nature intended. This is a very serious form of mass control and one which demands our immediate attention! We must watch everything that goes into our mouths and force our local politician to protect our food supply from these genetic engineering programs. By the way, our government passed a bill stating that these biotech companies do NOT have to tell us that what we are eating is a genetically modified or engineered food! We will cover this in later

books but in the meantime do your own
research!

The Spell Of Racism (White Supremacy)

The White supremacist or racist mentality, culture/behavior must be analyzed by the victims of racism, prior to reading any other perspective on such topic by another one else. Research all books on European thought/culture/behavior from first an African perspective. (See Yurugu, Isis Papers) This should not be done from hate, because they are still our family that came from us in the form of the albino melanin recessive gene that came from Africa allegedly. We need to breakdown that entire structure in order to understand the components of this particular construct we exist in, so we can heal this planet of ignorance in any and all areas it emerges from. Whether the ignorance emerges from

Blacks and the acceptance of the nigger mentality or White's in the form of White supremacy or racism neither exist for the betterment of humanity as a whole. The creature or beast of burden or social automaton that was created during slavery is not really us, but a virtual reality of us. By just thinking and postulating on the cure for these mentalities helps in that it releases a boundary that blocked those thought from even manifesting before. The slave self is defined here as the created, artificial man made social automaton called the nigger, which is a virtual self, produced as reactions to circumstances and situations engineered and created by White supremacy and religious enslavement. White supremacy and the nigger mentality is the problem on this planet today! We can sugar coat it or trivialize it at our own peril, but it is this mentality that has this world in the condition that it's in. Please don't be deceived into thinking the nigger mentality is just a black mentality. Please! White people, Asians, Arabs, Native Americans, Jews, and Gentiles all have this mentality. White supremacy has many gatekeepers from all races and ethnicities. This is a global issue as well as an individual battle. With these two powerful mentalities in place no one is immune from its effects. The white racial construct has spent centuries manipulating history, destroying historical records, using propaganda as a weapon, using slave labor, and using lies and deceit to continue to perpetuate and enforce its existence. White supremacy is a myth in itself. It's not real when you look behind the façade and illusion created to substantiate its existence. The white race is not God, the white race is not the chosen people, they are not the original people on this planet, and the white race is not the supreme race on the planet. This is simply not true yet subliminally and overtly enforced in every sector of society to give power to the Great Lie. Humanity do not be deceived! Let us unite in truth. If I tell a lie over and over again and have everyone else supporting and telling the same lie in their own way, what will we have? A massive lie being masqueraded as the truth! The truth is our history and legacy has been purposefully hidden, distorted and manipulated. Why were all the statues across Africa, and the world over, altered intentionally to attempt to hide its Afrikan features? This was an attempt to obviously hide the true authors of the pyramids and hieroglyphics as well as ancient temples all across this planet. The time has come for the truth to be told. We don't need the lies anymore. We cannot fall back asleep anymore. Our children need the true family tree to be shown to them and the correct photo album revealed now! Those photo albums are seen in the pyramids, hieroglyphics, and statues all around the world built by black people not aliens! Scientist have been confirmed Africa as the cradle of ALL humanity! A cradle is a crib where babies sleep. So all humanity owes its civilization and existence to Africa and it is time to pay homage.

These are questions for you to ponder on, research and discuss pertaining to **European culture/thought/behavior:**

1. How does the European world dominance continue to apparently break the natural cause and effect cycle or the karmic cycle? Meaning his exploitations of every single non White race on the planet earth is well known and documented throughout history, yet without seemingly a

lasting failure in his primary goal of dominance and manipulation.

2. How does the European avoid an all out attack against his White supremacist capitalistic system from all sides? Or can he avoid this?

3. Why is the European medical establishments still taken seriously when they have not allegedly found any cures for major diseases on this planet? Even though billions of dollars have already been invested in all this medical research for all these years, still no results?

4. Why are the European doctors still "practicing" medicine instead of curing people for real?

5. Is the fact that the medical system uses the term "practice" an admission to a lack of true knowledge pertaining to the causation of diseases and its cures?

6. Why doesn't the White culture on a whole if it is truly beyond the color issue or race issue, not speak out against racism or White supremacy publicly and expose the real mechanics of racism to help solve the problem?

7. Can you name one non White ethnic group that has not gotten into a conflict (war) with the Europeans at some point in history? What does that answer reveal?

8. Where did the White race come from or how did he come into existence since by there own admission the original people on the planet were Black? I need the White man to tell me where he came from, not us or our theory. I want to hear his own historical explanation on his true beginnings.

9. Will the White race ever come clean
    and tell the truth in terms of all the
    historical lies and misinformation on
    the Black race and our true
    contribution to humanity? Meaning
    the lies about religion's, prophets or
    messiahs being White, to all humans
    came from monkey's, to historical
    misrepresentations, to racism and all
    its components, etc.; will it ever be
    straighten out and addressed from a
    true spirit of forgiveness and
    reconciliation on their part ?

Europeans must believe that our coming
to the knowledge of self and the truth
about our past, his past and where he's
taking this planet, would mean and end
to his story. His very survival depends
on maintaining this spell.   If the
European were as superior as claimed
and truly see us as inferior, then why
are they so afraid to tell the truth in its

entirety and spend so much energy and money trying to keep us in a certain mind frame? It is because after years and years of studying us, they know indeed who we really are. It seems they would rather the nigger stand on the world stage then the liberated Afrikan. This is evident in what they show to the world through their propaganda, miseducation and programming. White supremacy must be replaced with actual facts and it must happen NOW! No more lies. Humanity wants and deserves the truth, so we can live in harmony with each other as it should be.

Spell Of The Master/Student Relationship

The problem with the master/student relationship arises "within yourself" when you lose who **you** are in relation to your teacher and mistake the master existing externally (the teacher) as the Lord, or Savior and not a reflection of the true master to be which has always been you! This **is** your world and we are in your world as reflections of the many forms, lessons, and tests that your higher self reveals to you, in order for you to graduate out of this plane of existence and into higher conscious realms. This must be deeply overstood! Of course to each person the same statement is true so there is no need to ego trip or lose yourself in the glory of your own existence. We are all connected and interrelated and placed in each other's lives at specific times to help each other either grow, remain stagnate or go backwards in life. Of course we love, honor and deeply respect our elders or the master teachers, and we should; however when we worship and over emphasize the teacher or your reflections, you never get to be in union with yourself and will always feel fragmented from reality. **YOU ARE THE REALITY!** This is like looking into an ocean and seeing the reflections of yourself and all the things around you and then living your life looking into the water at the reflections and calling that your reality. It looks real but there is a distortion in the reflection when looking into the water. Images do not appear clearly and you still feel different, isolated, and separate from those figures floating in the water. The only way to snap out of that false sense of reality is to become aware of who is actually standing above the water looking down at these reflections, **YOU!** And the things you see in the reflection are around **YOU!** Again do not get egotistical or become an ego statistic, I'm not talking about the "you" that's been programmed by this matrix, your environment, religion, etc, but the higher universal self. The self that perceives the unity with everything and yet is none of it! This is the "you" where the kingdom of heaven is said to reside, which is the deeper aspect of the self. All this perception we're speaking about is not with the two physical eyes, but with the symbolic third eye, which is the inner mind's eye. The whole science of magic tricks and mind manipulation are built on illusions whether optical or mental. The ancient masters worldwide never taught certain truths openly or in public because of the fear that this knowledge might fall into the hands of human demons who will use this knowledge to control, manipulate and destroy the righteous and the truth on earth. Sadly enough this is exactly what has happened and our "fall" from our divine state was predicted by our ancestors' years ago in ancient Kemet and our rebirth and rise was predicted as well. This information which was only for the initiate in ancient Kemet must now be dispensed to our people worldwide because it has already reached the hands of the unrighteous and is being used by them to create mischief and confusion on this planet. These individuals that used our knowledge in attempts to enslave and subjugate the world inhabitants deceive only themselves in the end because the Grandmasters of our ancestors already defeated them and solved the negative equation of self, through Supreme mathematics, science and conscious elevation! **The battle has already been won!** That's why it said in

Revelations that Michael and his angels fought against the dragon and his angels and the dragon prevailed not!" This *is* spiritual warfare **FIRST** which subsequently manifest itself onto the physical plane. We didn't lose the war family! But **we must choose our sides consciously, to fight for and protect that which matters most.** Interesting to note that the word "now" backwards is won! **The battle is won now! Choose your side. Accept your destiny! Manifest your true reality!** It is interesting to note that American slave traders forced the original Black family during slavery to call them "master". Why? First of all, these men, the controllers and architects of the slave trade were in fact freemasons. These men knew that we were the real masters but chose to purposefully deceive our ancestors and their children into accepting them as authority figures and gods. These men were examples of why the original masters refused to teach them the high sciences and mathematics because of their weak and wicked nature and lack of self control. These slave traders, like the Arab slave traders were examples why our ancient ancestors only carefully selected disciples or students to initiate into these orders of universal knowledge because of the dangers this knowledge possesses if fallen into the wrong hands. These men only could reach 33 degrees within the knowledge of self, thus there knowledge is still vastly incomplete and unfulfilled. They are still looking to us to fill in the blanks for them. They succumbed to their weak lower animal nature and resorted to stealing the mystic knowledge and utilizing it against the dark original nations. So these men knew the psychological implications the word "master" had, because remember family they called our ancestors master and Gods for hundreds of years, as we taught and civilized all the nations of the earth. This is not a belief or superstition or wishful thinking, this is the historical facts that the White race never truly denied; they just chose not to speak on it, place this history in any state sponsored school system, nor elaborate on its meaning and implication! Now, the way we prepare ourselves to eventually master our own existence and destiny is to become seekers of knowledge, wisdom and overstanding and become students of life to then qualify ourselves as Gods and masters, rather than followers or servants. Let me breakdown the mind of a Seeker/Student vs. the Mind of the Follower/Servant.

Mind of a Seeker/Student

1. The seeker seeks a supreme overstanding of the Universal Self.
2. The Seeker/Student seeks to intuitively comprehend reality. To live reality.
3. The Seeker/Student seeks to become one with Self (Universe, others, reality).
4. The Seeker/Student can meditate, reflect and contemplate truth from any and all sources, taking none on face value.
5. The Seeker/Student learns about Self to eventually master self and its positive and negative aspects. Destiny becomes the lessons learned.
6. The Seeker/Student becomes a Universal holistic thinker.
7. The Seeker/Student perceives reality as through the eyes of "God".

8. The Seeker/Student masters self and the universe.
9. The Seeker/Student has the inner strength, love, and confidence to challenge ideas, concepts, and realities given to them.

Mind of the Follower

1. The follower wants supreme knowledge of a doctrine or dogma.
2. The follower wants to just intellectualize reality and religion rather than live it and/or become it.
3. The follower wants group superiority and uniqueness and isolates others.
4. The follower memorizes a doctrine or dogma with a closed mind and can only listen to their teacher's teachings. Localized mind state.
5. The follower practices dogmatic regurgitation.

6. The follower sees reality only through the eyes of their master or religion.

7. The follower succumbs to the spell easily and loves to surrender their thinking/behavior to religion, White supremacy, and other's view on reality.

8. The follower masters nothing significant.

9. The follower follows continually.

To place your mind and soul in the hands of any entity, person, religion, or group without being allowed to exercise critical thinking and common sense is mental and spiritual suicide.

Religion as a Spell

The most famous question asked when you begin to talk about life, history, or anything involving causation in people's experience will be, "What religion are you"? The most interesting thought about this question is the hidden implication of, "Which man's thoughts recorded do you accept as true"? Also the question implies that you've even made a choice between these ideas. The fact of the matter is you were given a religion to believe in at birth depending on where you were born, whether it is Christianity, Islam, or Judaism. These were given to you to believe in by your family first whom you love and trust. Your family received this information from society or I should say the ruling class of conquerors. Any research into the origin of the three

131

major religions will reveal there is a founder for each one. The true seeker will research further than the religion given to them by those that invaded their culture, to discover what their people believed in or practiced spiritually prior to the coming of Judaism, Christianity, or Islam? My point here is there is no exclusive group, or person on the planet earth that has some monopoly on life's meaning and journey. Of course we have individuals who have raised their consciousness to the level where they're able to teach and inform others on what they have learned. This is a fact that we utilize our elder's knowledge to build on from what we have now. The word "master" in ancient times was a title given to the man that reached a level of self control (controlling the animal desires) through self discipline and self knowledge by way of trial and error, experiences, tests, victories and failures. These self mastered individuals in ancient Kemet (Egypt) were appointed as judges of the people's affairs and organizers of society, due to their level of spiritual maturity, self sacrifice and devotion to the principles of truth and justice. The huge difference between our ancestors yesterday as rulers and these men today as modern day rulers is that the men of today, are *not* spiritual masters nor do they strive to be. A judge should be the most wise and righteous man in his society, not someone who got a law degree from a "prestigious" university or joined some secret society to become chosen to be a judge. No! These judges are by far not righteous and this is the problem with our society. Nobody personifies the true meaning of the service their profession demands. Same principles apply to these medical doctors, who aren't really healing anyone in a holistic manner, by addressing the person as a whole and total being. These doctors are drug pushers pushing the latest FDA approved drug from these pharmaceutical companies that wine and dine these doctors or hospital administrators to sell their drugs. These people are not real doctors' family! They are only practicing medicine, and they are not in the business of curing diseases that's for sure. The proof is in the results or I should say no results. These people only "practice" medicine and law because of the money, status, and long term benefits. That's it! Neither doctors nor scientist have used their collective brain power and knowledge to **solve** any diseases we've been confronted with for centuries now! In ancient times people looked to ancient masters for guidance on the spiritual path, for healing advice and remedies and to help manage their affairs, because they (the masters) accomplished the true goal of life or what every conscious being should be striving for; **the mastery of self**. These same masters were worshipped and revered and placed on a pedestal in their society and seen as a divine deity. Upon their deaths these people's names were called on or used to invoke spiritual power, to heal or protect them throughout their lives. These ancient ones were the first Gods or Christ on earth and subsequently their stories of knowledge and healing spread across this planet, to later be turned into mythological stories used by religion. A good example of this is our Kemetic or Egyptian elder Imhotep, who of course was a Black man and the true father of medicine. He's the brother that Hippocrates studied, who is credited with being the father of Western medicine. Study Imhotep from a Black source if you want the true story, then go to a White source to compare, not validate, if you choose. Some masters were guides and teachers to those seekers on the path of self mastery and discovery by their many lessons and examples. While other masters went into seclusion and established secret societies initiating a chosen few in the principles of self mastery and universal knowledge. No individual living on this planet has gained knowledge of self on their own. Even the animals and nature itself are master teachers in that its very existence reflects our true nature if contemplated in silent observation. Observation of animal behavior or the functions and changes in nature reveals truths if you're open and reflective mentally and there you can find the mystery of life revealed. No one arrives at the level of mastery without some guidance along the way or at some point in their development.

Religion as a social control instrument has been well documented across the globe, yet its effects remain powerful and its influence is lasting. Religion is used as a tool to divide and conquer us by first presenting allegorical intuitive spirituality and its meaning and making it historical events. This places you outside the meaning of the story in its purest form and reduces this knowledge to a mundane level, in which you see characters, which should represent spiritual ideals within you to strive for, as actual historical characters to distance yourself from, and not become. That's why in Christianity it is all about accepting Jesus as your "personal Lord and Savior" instead of "picking up your cross and follow me" or follow my path or become what your waiting for to come. Earlier "religions" such as Buddhism and Hinduism knew that the path to enlightenment or spirituality existed within you as your own struggle over your carnal self not believing someone came to save you from this work. Jesus himself says the "kingdom of heaven is within" so why are you looking to go somewhere else? The spell of religion was cast on us as a means to control our thinking and behavior. This spell is how a slave owner could go to church and even be the pastor, yet have slaves and not sense a contradiction in this. This split between church and state or your state of being was a tool used to divide man up internally, so as to justify anything they do in the name of God that differs from the racist laws they create and enforce. So religion is in one box, and the law is in another. Yet when you go to court you have to swear on the Bible! What contradictions this spell contains! This is also why the image of Jesus is portrayed as White, like Krishna, even though his name literally means Black! From a White supremacist viewpoint, they had to get us to see Jesus and other spiritual characters as White because if they are White then "God" must be White as well. This is how your rational and intuitive mind sees this, whether you believe it or not. This belief that Jesus or Krishna or Muhammad was White manifest itself as an inferiority complex and a disconnectedness from racism as it is practiced, because you begin to feel you deserve to be a second class citizen or a slave. Subliminally we've been taught to worship the White male image as authoritative. In your thinking he's "God" and the Jews are the chosen people and they are White also, so your mind justifies their false reality and gives power to their false claims on the world stage. Even though in Revelations, Jesus says he knows the blasphemy of those that say they are Jews but are not or do lie!! Who could he be talking about if we historically can establish that the original "Jews" or Hebrew people were Black? The fact of the matter is that this was a religious spell placed on the minds of Black people and the world. Jesus was never a White man symbolically, mythological, or literally! God or god is not, nor ever was a White man! That was all lies and manipulation, which every Easter and Christmas the tell lies vision (television) continues to enforce without any protest. The "Jews" today are admittedly called the "modern day Israelis" not the biblical Jews, who were said to be the Hebrew people of the Old Testament. The people called Jews today know that they are not those Jews but we do not. This research into the origin of Israel and who the true Jews are can be easily obtained yet not researched, because the spell keeps you from looking. This is not hate or disrespect to any "Jew" but just the historical truth as even they know it. The Black man and women was the original people on the planet earth and so the Creator of man in "his" image could not be anything but Black also. The White race, our children, have used the lie of changing images to theirs and manipulating history and lying about our past and theirs, to appease their own feelings of racial inferiority. If they would just admit they came from Blacks and want to know how they look so different then us, just ask that question?

That is what all this genome project and genetic research is really all about. Discovering his past and trying to master a race of people. We are not in competition with the White race nor any other race for that matter once we all establish the truth. I say to the great, great, great, grandchildren of those slave owners that are now benefiting from lies, enslavements, and mass deception that your overall silence on these issues speaks volumes as to where your heart really is. You are still participating in what has been labeled modern day slavery. Today's new slave system in which you have been given the controls to, and yet you utter not a word to your Black family members struggling under the yoke of White supremacy by offering up your knowledge, your voice and your understanding to our situation, like some of your forefathers did in the struggle to end slavery. You remind me of the type of White person that borrow our culture when its convenient for you, i.e. wearing Bob Marley T-shirts, have African masks in your house, dress in culture clothing and even wear locks or some culture style, yet when you see a real Black man or women exhibiting his culture in either dress or speech, you have nothing to say! I've seen White dudes walking around wearing dreads and do their best to imitate Afrikan culture yet not speak or hail up the Blacks who look like the image they emulate? That's pseudo!! That's fake and insincere and yes I'm calling you out! As far as your real involvement in our struggle besides wearing the costumes, why not write your own book on how to end racism or expose the racial construct, or open up your own center or program yourself without having to join a work already in progress, then get mad when you're not welcomed. You're not welcomed most of the time because it is not sincere. You offer nothing to the table as to your perspective on the solution to White supremacy within this country and the world, coming from a White "insiders" perspective. What most of you do is leech off the Black struggle to advance your own platform or agenda whether it is gay rights, White women's liberation, or animal rights. You can save these animals and speak out on their injustice and cruelty with passion, yet do not say anything to help your Black family members battle against White supremacy, legalized racism, police brutality, etc. It is all hypocrisy! You Whites who stay silent in this day and time are afraid to speak out against racism do so because you actually do not want to see it end. You feel you benefit from it, which you really do not, and do not want to see the full truth emerge. That's why I challenge anyone to name a White entertainer or celebrity that speaks out verbally and articulately on racism and how it is practiced in this country. Who? You're not challenging the system because you're fake and insincere and feel safe in the arms of White supremacy. Shame on you! Your soul will bear witness to this one day. Electing Obama is a start in the acceptance of the Black male image, yet you are unable to stomach the actual process of dismantling centuries of legal racial constructs, revisiting past aggressions to heal, and dealing with what the revolutionary symbolism of a Black man historically rising to this stature can really mean.

Life is not something to be explained away through mere intellectualizing and acknowledging. You must strive to live and become God not merely worshippers of the concept as it exist outside of yourself. Jesus said the kingdom of heaven is within right? And where do they say God resides? In heaven! So where is God if heaven is within? Please think about that! Why perceive your life and destiny through the eyes of another except to learn and observe their examples and lessons and apply these to our experience? When you rigidly attach yourself to a doctrine or belief, you are on the road to stagnation! You become stuck! This stagnation results in your inability to think or exist apart or outside of your master, leader, teacher or religions viewpoint. You have the right to break the mold and be an original thinker. You have free access to the essence, if you are sincere and attempting to live a

145

righteous life. All is available to you. If we ever want true freedom, justice and equality for the original family and all other oppressed races on earth, then we as the true 5% of the population must stand up and be the Gods and Goddesses this world has been looking and waiting for! The "mother ship" is the unity of our being. One aim, one goal, and one destiny! We are the knowledge! The knowledge exists in us. It exists in our very cells and inside of our DNA and outside of our DNA! We are condensed molecular vibration chained to this physical world through magnetism. Release your spirit from bondage without fear! Manifest now! Only characters in this "game of life" are interchangeable not the content of the story. So do not get hung up on the characters, but look deeper into the meaning of the story. You are divine or can become divine when you purify your heart and refine your mind, intent and actions.

Do not preach religion, become the spirit of the true idea of the religion. Do not believe in righteousness become righteous! **Sometime ago "God" must have existed as Satan also to show and prove the mastery and knowledge of all degrees of Self.** How else can evil have come into existence, if God didn't bring it into existence? Nothing exist independent of God's creation right? We must overstand this concept and balance. Live as righteous as you can, but do not be deceived! There is a time and place for everything, even war! Do not be deceived in what righteousness means! This is true overstanding here. Our African brothers and sisters created Kung fu or martial arts so they won't have to fight or kill someone out of fear, but to protect their peace. However, if you overstepped your boundary then you had to be dealt with, and that's called justice. You are the sole controller of your universe if you want to be. I know this is a big responsibility and a little scary (maybe a lot scary!) but that's who we are! You see family, pimps are controllers of women, and politicians are manipulators of the weak, innocent and infantile minds. Pimps use women to build a financial empire for themselves without really giving anything in return. Open your mind. Do not be a hooker in life! P.T. Barnum said, a sucker is born every minute, and how many minutes are in a single day, yet alone years? How many fools and zombies roam the streets of your city or town? The spiritual world has pimps and hookers as well. Yes family, preachers prostituting your desire to find yourself and go to "heaven", yet give you fantasy and mythology in the place of true empowerment. If Jesus said not to store up for yourself treasures on this earth, explain how come these preachers have so much treasure? If you are truly fighting the

148

"devil's system" why are you able to prosper so mightily in it? It is all game, and there are those that can see how obvious these **spiritual pimps** are! If I can fish and you were never taught how to fish nor have the desire to learn, and we live in a world surrounded by water, who will rule? Who will be the master and who will be the slave? This is the mentality of capitalism, monopolies and the economic survival of the fittest. Unfortunately the Black race has been conquered because we lost the knowledge of true reality and were taught myths in its place. We were allowed to come to the Monopoly game after they played for 5 hours. We have no property and are just rolling dice, going to jail and paying rent. Think about that! We lost the reality of self and life's true meaning. We were tricked into believing rather than knowing what is going on around us and inside of us. Religion made us stupid because we accepted the mystery god concept rather than taking matters of life into our own hands and making this world the heaven it is suppose to be! **We have been placed under a spell that has us waiting for something or someone else to change this world instead of us!** What a clever design to keep things the way they are? It is similar to the Wizard of Oz story, where the wizard is just an ordinary man trying to get back home, but creates an illusion called Oz. This "man" has a following of people that he used to build a temple for him, and created an image of God, I mean Oz, for them to look to and be kept in fear of. They knew not to challenge the Great and Powerful Oz. Same thing with the God concept upon closer examination. When will we wake up from the poppy fields and see the truth? We must regain our minds and souls from these spiritual vampires seeking to rob us of our vitality and life force and to prevent us from regaining our rightful place again. People will kill someone to defend a religious doctrine and still feel that they are righteous and justified in doing so. That's how deep the spell goes! Instead of searching out the truth or proving the person wrong, would rather kill someone that challenges their spell. I can learn from all religions because I can extract universal truths from dogma and mythology. I do not have to hate you because you may disagree with my opinion or interpretations. And I do not have to accept your mythology anymore than you have to accept the historicity of Apollo, Zeus, Thor, or the Hulk! They're many leaders who sacrificed their lives to give the original nation of Africans a sense of pride, restore true history and a blueprint of our glorious past, to create our glorious future. **The real blueprint! When we sit together at the table of brother and sisterhood**

and iron out our differences and focus on our strengths and common plights, we will have the greatest nation of people ever known to man at anytime in history! This is what our future can be if we want it to be that way. The other alternative is either perpetual enslavement or an extinction level event for humanity. Those are the choices**. We as a people have a choice on whether we will accept a computer generated dream world or chose a new one.** After we survive this hell, we as a people, who have been victims of slavery, self destruction, self hate, and racism, will rise from the ashes like a Phoenix and rule for the next millennium. All of our great visionaries seen this before they died, why can't we? We are nothing if we're scattered and separated. That old divide and conquer game is old and played! Stop falling for the same tricks. No more I'm living large while my brother lives small.

Now it is "How do I help bring out your talents, ideas and passions to aid the whole nation, not just your tribe?" This is the goal. Anything less is division and manipulation and you know it. With the knowledge we have now its no more excuses. We must begin to apply the science and math! Get off your high horse you so called Black leaders and come down to earth and let's communicate with each other on the real solutions for our people. If negative forces can come together to plot and plan to ensure their future, then what the hell is our "leaders" problem? Is it the ego? Please brothers and sisters do not let another 1000 years pass because you were trying to collect riches from this beast system at the expense of revealing truth to your people! There are so many of us with serious agendas and mind power, along with ancestral spiritual power, so the time is now. **This day I will call "Dawn of the Dead",**

because we were once dead in the moon cycle of ignorance only to see the dawn of the promised sun cycle of light and intelligence. We must awake to the highest potential shown in Kemet to a living deity. Signs and symbols have never been the true reality. Hieroglyphics, holy books, spoken words, etc. are all external guides for the inner world where the truth lies. These are mere guides or maps for the inner meaning these symbols seek to express and represent. To attempt to find meaning in these symbols outside of you is to search for fool's gold. In the most ancient Pyramids the carving "Know thyself" or Knowledge of Self is inscribed. The pyramids were one of the highest achievements of the Black man/woman and the highest achievement for any race for that matter. And no the pyramids were not built from slavery like you were taught, and no, the "aliens" did not build the pyramids either! Our ancestors did! The White man knows this and he hides this achievement by trying to insinuate that some extraterrestrials built the pyramids, even though he says that aliens do not exist! This is another clever way to discredit ancient Afrikans and cast doubt on an issue that should be obvious and all that it implies concerning the architects of the pyramids. We must be the aliens then because we built the pyramids you see all over the world! Like brother Bobby Hemmitt said, the pyramids and hieroglyphics were created by our ancestors because they knew the White race was going to come into power and we were going to fall asleep to the knowledge of ourselves. So these pyramids and hieroglyphics were the reminder of our legacy, our past and future that would reawaken our genetic memory. To just blueprint this type of structure shows and proves the magnificent mind and spirit of our people. Kemetic (Egyptian) people created our whole society based on the physical, mental and spiritual qualities and potential in our people. Take a look at a subway map or road map and you're witnessing veins and human arteries displayed, but substituted for highways and trains. Look at it. The temple is in us! This was how our ancient society was built and this is how we will rebuild it! **My point in dealing with this Spell of Religion is that no exclusive religion or faith or doctrine has the only truth to reach the source of it all.** And if you are looking for a religion, then you certainly wouldn't be looking at any Johnny come lately religion in today's time. You would have to go back to Afrika to find that religion. **Living the true reality of self is religion in its purest form.** When babies are born and before you as parents enforce a belief system on them, notice the peace, the bliss, the sincerity,

156

and the innocence without your religion. **Among all these religions that are on the planet today, how are we to determine or are expected to determine which one is the right one?** How do you or did you arrive at which religion was the truth? **Did you honestly investigate every single religion and spiritual practice on the planet before you made your decision to accept one as "the truth"?** In Christianity, if you do not accept Jesus as your personal Lord and Savior at some point in your life and live as a "Christian", then hell fire awaits you. In Islam, if you do not accept Muhammad as the final prophet sent from "Allah", and accept Islam as your religion, you can forget about heaven, as hell awaits you. Not to mention that each of these two religions are broken off into hundreds of sects or subgroups, all claiming they represent the "truth". Who's right? Both religions say you are going to hell if you do

157

not choose them! So with all these decisions to make and the repercussions being so severe, where does one turn? Turn to Jesus you say, because you were born in this country that taught their version of Christianity as the nation's religion? Turn to Islam you say, because the White man lied to you about Christianity and gave you their religion when your real religion is Islam. Didn't the Arab give you that religion as well Black man? No? **You can not turn to an organized religion and say, "I've found it, the true religion!" and then when someone comes along and proves what you were believing is a version of truth mixed with outright lies, and blatant contradictions, you seek to evade these discussions and choose to go with whatever makes you feel safe.** What makes you feel safe is going along with the invaders or colonialist religion that has power over your society and way of life.

Don't do that? Do not let your fears determine your spiritual path? **That's the way Islam and Christianity was made to be the powerful religions they are today. Under the threat and fear of death our people converted to these religions.** The fear of death was physical then, and it is mental now. Let's face it family these religions are both fear based religions that use hell to get you to join. But my question is since they both threaten you with hell, how do you choose one hell over the other? **If your religious beliefs fail the test of authenticity, it is your obligation to elevate from that mind state.** Jesus in your Bible did not preach a religion. Jesus never said to accept him as your personal savior. Jesus never built churches with his 12 friends, being that he was a carpenter, he could have right? Why not? That's something to think about. But the Spell of Religion has you where you would rather sit

159

back comfortably in a church or mosque and say this dialogue to yourself: "Boy, I'm sure glad God or Allah sent so and so to save me from having to actually think for me. I'm glad because so and so came I can be saved and free from all responsibilities of my own actions. I'm so glad I do not have a mind of my own to use as I might see fit! I'm really glad I gave my heart to so and so because if this should backfire or prove not to be what they said it would be...then...If this isn't the true religion in the end then, it is not my fault, right? I mean I'm not to be blamed. I trusted so and so to be who they said they were! I mean why would somebody lie about something so serious as God or religion, you know, so it must be true? Right? Well I believe in God anyway so, that should be enough, right? I am really confused and scared about all this! I do not know what to believe, life seems so unfair, so one sided! No, yes I do! This is the true religion. Yeah, the devil is trying to win me over. Ha! Ha! I got you now devil, um where do I get baptized quickly before I change my mind again, please!" I'm not listening to anyone except Pastor so and so, or Bishop so and so, Reverend so and so or Imam so and so, so you can not make me doubt! Oh God somebody help me! I'm so lost and confused! Who or what do I believe in?" This dramatization is a mental skit all too familiar, which is played out in all religious minds at some point or another when the contradictions of their beliefs get challenged. I have a small suggestion my family to offer, why not start believing in ourselves! The creator that exists within us! I'm not endorsing narcissism or atheism, but I do know that you were blessed with a unique gift of your own. Your ability to think, reason, act and react within your own consciousness apart from others makes you unique. You have your own mind, not a herd's mind, but an individual mind capable of making sound decisions. Why are we so scared to live in our natural state and lifestyle which is conducive to peace, harmony and success? **You can tell these religions are spells because if they really had the truth like they all claim, then why is this world in the condition that it is in and we have all these religions? This devil wouldn't have anyplace to live because this planet would be filled with spirituality, love and peace! But in the midst of all these religions nothing but division and chaos are present. The proof is in the facts not words or opinions. We would be in a world of truth and justice if these religions really had the answers. Not the confusion created by ignorance, fear and lies.** The only reason you are confused within yourself is because of early programming and indoctrination called, **"Operation Fear of Self"**. Instead of seeking that kingdom of heaven within, we cling to a person to save us from the responsibility of solving our problems or the world's problems ourselves. Nice try but that's not going to work. **That's why a lot of religious people do not take the saving the planet earth thing seriously, because they have been programmed to let the earth be destroyed in the name of an apocalypse.** A baby needs their parents to pick them up when they're in an emotionally dependent state. So spiritually we want some religion to pick us up so we can feel safe in its promises for us. That's a false sense of security and when that religion puts you down, you cry until another religion picks you back up again. Hopefully we will make it to the point where we'll say, "Wait a minute, I can take the positive aspects of any religion and apply these principles to

163

my life. I can understand the negative as a learning experience and balance myself in harmony". This, my family, is called Maat in Kemet. This is not just manipulating yourself, although you do that in accepting these religions as the "truth". This is living in the reality of self, which is our culture's true religion or way of life. Give honor to your higher power and express your divine principles through rituals if you like. **We are the religion and way of life, because if we weren't here or didn't exist then what are we talking about…Nothing!**

10 Questions To Ask God?

1. **Why did you create evil?**
Meaning how did all good manifest anything evil to begin with? Or how could negativity come into existence if God didn't create it. People say God didn't create evil the devil did, and then I ask them did the devil create his own nature independent of God? What could be created without the Creator, evil included or even the ability to do evil?

2. **Why do not you just destroy the Devil immediately?**
According to Christianity and Islam, God is all powerful. So my question points to God using his

165

power without any delay. Why the delay in taking this evil force out of our lives?

3. **Why can't the Devil repent if he was a righteous angel in the beginning according to Christian folklore?** Help me understand how can someone as righteous as Lucifer was said to be according to folklore never finds it in himself to admit he was wrong. How righteous was he then?

4. **Why don't you convert the Devil back to a positive angel and balance this whole equation?** Wouldn't that be the most beautiful of endings? The Devil turns back good again and

the universe is restored to its glorious beginning. But then revenge wouldn't be able to take place against all the wrongs he's done now would it?

5. **If you're a jealous God, how many other Gods are out there that is seen as competition for you?**

6. **How can you be jealous of something you created?** Last time I checked, Jealousy is a trait of the Devil and weakness?

7. **If you are in fact everywhere, all powerful, and all knowing, then you are intentionally allowing things to happen knowing the results. Why are**

you doing this? What is this drama called life really all about?

8. **If this battle between good and evil is really about Satan and you, why are we involved in this drama at all?**

9. **In the Bible and Quran you say you get jealous, angry, revengeful, feel sorry you created man, and other human emotions, why do you seem to be going through the same emotions we have if you are God?**

10. **Will you send one of your children to hell because they didn't join a particular religion, even if they tried their best to**

be righteous and have a good heart?

I asked these questions from the perspective of the God concept according to the Bible and Koran. If the creator of the universe and life as we know it exists as the character in these books, then these are some of the questions I would ask. These questions are not designed to be disrespectful toward anyone's concept of God, but to stimulate thought on the implications each question reveals. If a child can and does ask us questions about life and God, then we should be able to ask thought provoking questions without feeling afraid or judged?

Breaking the Hypnotic Trance Without the Hypnotist!

Usually when a person is placed under a hypnotic spell, there minds have been hijacked for lack of a better word and the hypnotist is in control of this person's mind, manipulating them like a puppet. This is shown in television shows and written in books since the 1950's. You've seen people made to bark like dogs or do some other demeaning act as a demonstration of the power the hypnotist has over their subjects mind and behavior. Of course these talk shows dramatize these hypnotic subjects and use actors, but the principle of someone influencing your mind through hypnosis has been researched and its effects known for over 50 years at least! Some people are much more susceptible and vulnerable to being hypnotized then others; however if placed in a constant bombardment of hypnotic suggestions, even the strong minded person can crack eventually, if they are not constantly fortifying themselves with empowering suggestions. As I've said earlier, if you're watching television and not challenging every image presented to your mind on a conscious level, then you are being hypnotized and your behavior is being controlled and altered. When you go out to the store to buy that product you've been watching on television all day or week, you will think you are making that decision, but you're not! You've been hypnotized into making the decision to purchase that product through a clever mind control technique called "subliminal advertisement". This same theory works with selling you pharmaceutical products of drugs. The advertisements for the drug list all these symptoms and ask you the viewer, have you experienced any one or more of these symptoms. They know that most people are weak minded and are easily persuaded, so when most people see a symptom that everyone at some point in their lives experience, they might automatically assume they have the disease they advertised and thus need to buy that product. This is called auto suggestion, and is another powerful weapon of mind control used to sell you drugs. This same technique is what the fear of these viruses cause, and the person feels compelled to get a vaccine or inoculation from a supposed disease that never existed before, but now mysteriously exist. They have a new epidemic or disease coming up daily and this is a form of casting a spell on our minds to have us become drug addicts for some drug company's product. Not to mention the deadly side effects listed in their commercials that are as bad as or worse than what you're taking the drug for! Notice how fast the person stating the side effects is talking in these commercials. They do not want you to analyze these side effects clearly because then you might not buy their product. They also hypnotize you with the side effects being brought into your awareness so fast that you didn't have time to analyze, thus programming your mind to internalize those side effects. People are interrelated and influence each other naturally. That's why when one person yawns someone else yawns as well. This is what these companies and advertisers know and use against us, to convince ourselves that we are sick with whatever symptom the commercial outlined.

Normally the only way to break a hypnotic trance is through the hypnotist. Remember in the movies, the hypnotist counts back from ten to one and then his subject would become conscious again or back in control of their own mind, yet forgetting the whole experience of their minds being hijacked. **But what if the hypnotist does not snap you out of it? What if you were perpetually left in a trance or a hypnotic state?** You would be walking around doing the bidding of the hypnotist until either he frees you (and why on earth would he do that?) or dies and his influence loses power, or you free yourself from the hypnotic lock placed on your consciousness. Sounds familiar? **Are you under a Spell?** Just because a person hypnotized appears to be in control of their minds, doesn't mean they are in control of all of their minds! They could be hypnotized in a particular area of there consciousness, that certain trigger words or sounds brings them under a trance. Here are some ways to break the hypnotic trance without help from the hypnotist: When you are walking around, notice your breathing pattern. Focus on deliberate, long full breathes as you walk or stand. While traveling in your vehicle, or on public transportation practice deep breathing. Try to get to 1 to 2 breaths a minute. Now, when someone approaches you, do you stop breathing or suspend your breath or change breathing patterns? You're being placed in a hypnotic trance at that moment. Focus now on continuing your breathing as you were doing before that person arrived. You are now engaging the trance state consciously. A big part of any trance or hypnotic state is to operate outside of your conscious awareness, thus it is designed to place you in an automatic response mode, which is not what you want. You want to become aware of how you're reacting to things around you.

For example, when a person comes into your presence become aware of how you are breathing and how your body language changes as a result of their presence. Slow everything down mentally. Do you feel how you automatically want to go into another position and alter your breathing? Or are you attempting to alter your posture or facial structure? Become aware of this. **You're fighting the trance at the life force level, which is contained in the breath.** Notice yourself and what you hold unconsciously in your hands such as tissue, keys, money or whatever. Notice after or during a deep thought or a mental breakthrough there is a big distraction i.e. the phone rings, loud noise occurs, someone calls you, yelling, loud laughter or talking, your own body may begin to twitch or itch, someone touches you, you get the chills, you feel sick in your stomach or your ears may have a crawling sensation.

177

Begin to record your dreams by keeping a dream journal and write down what you remember in detail about your dream as soon as you wake up. Have a pen and pad right besides the bed. Do not wait! Record any animals present, places, colors, things seen or experienced, feelings and people involved, also record overall theme of your dreams. Special study subjects include but are not limited to: **Distractions** (We covered some here), **Hypnotics, Spells, Sleep, Dreams, Emotions, Brainwashing Techniques, Psycho Somatic responses, and Meditation.**

In terms of distraction analysis the key question to ask yourself is what were you doing, thinking about or saying "before" you were distracted? There are words that cause a physical/ mental (psychosomatic) reaction or response in you. What are those trigger words? These are the words or phrases that set you off or cause you to go into an automatic reaction mode of thinking and/or behaving. Learn those words for yourself and master the energy these words elicit in you through diffusion meditation.

How much are we creating with our own thoughts? We create our reality largely, yet if we are under a hypnotic spell our reality has been hijacked by the hypnotist. So are we really creating our own reality under those circumstances? Not until we break the hypnotic trance lock can we truly create our own reality. **Are distractions a method to keep us from believing in ourselves or questioning our natural responses and impulses? As your reading this, what major distraction is happening right Now? What distractions have occurred throughout this reading?**

Phenomena alert is the phenomena or things happening around you simultaneously as you become aware of a truth happening at that moment. Notice when in strict concentration on a goal any interruption that seeks to derail your train of thought. Upon being seen at 1st sight or upon entering a building or when entering into the presence of a group of people, what is there first reaction upon seeing you? What is your initial vibe telling you? These are a few ways you will begin to break the hypnotic trance lock without help from the hypnotist. Your initial vibe is of course tainted to a large degree depending on your own mind state, current emotional level, and conscious elevation, so you have to process your vibe accordingly. However when forced to make a quick assessment you should trust your initial vibe as the truth, even if it is only true for that moment. This is a layperson's guide to understanding the

180

spell we are currently under and battling to elevate from. It is up to you to further your research into theories and terminologies posted on the internet and written in books. I encourage you to study as much as you can to master the information, but remember all the websites and books in the world mean nothing if we are not going to put these theories into practice. What I gave you is an introduction into the concept in terms that are easy to understand for the beginner on the journey of self mastery and self realization. This information is also for the individual already on the path and in need of some encouragement and further validation to their own intuitive knowledge. This book was written straight from the heart and I hope it helps you in whatever way you deem necessary. As always, it is my honor and privilege to serve you in my humble capacity as your brother and friend and most important to help elevate my

Afrikan people's conscious state first and subsequently all human beings truly seeking higher enlightenment. Peace and love to you all!

Ambassador Ausar

Visit **blogtalkradio.com/ambassadorausar**

For a LIMITED time only for Ambassaor Ausar's BlogTalkRadio Show Archives

Spiritual Analysis of Dreams

Consciousness of Food

African American Food Crisis: What's Left to eat? Special Guest Sister Manana

Mind Control Through Foods: Special Guest Dr. Phil Valentine

Analysis of the God Concept Part 1: "Search for the Mystery God"

Is Hip Hop the New Counter Intelligence Program? Special Guest Black Dot

Do We REALLY Need Weed? A Critical Analysis of Marijuana in the Afrikan Community

Our Sacred Treasure: Analysis of the Black Family

Blueprint for Black Power: Nation Building 101: Special Guest Sara Suten Seti

Ambassador Ausar Interviews Hashim
Nzinga: National Chief of Staff of the New
Black Panther Party

SPIRITUAL PIMPS: Analysis of Prosperity
Theology and the Manipulation of Spiritual
Concepts

The Abduction and Possession of Afrikan
Consciousness: Special Guest Dr. Phil
Valentine

13 Year Anniversary Hip Hop Special:
Analysis of the Musical Influence of Biggie
Smalls

African Presence in Asia Including the
Arabian Peninsula: Special Guest Ronoko
Rashidi

Black To Our Roots: Pan-African
Community Organization Habesha, Inc.

African Origin of Islam w/ special guest Dr.
Wesley Muhammad

Analysis of the Teachings and Mission of Dr.
Malachi Z. York

Why is that? The Whitewashing of African
History and the Creation of Historical
Amnesia

184

Are We Really Living In The Last Days On Earth?

The Real State of the Afrikan Union Address with Ambassador Ausar

African Holistic Healing "One Year Anniversary Special"

Black Infant Mortality: Why are our babies dying?

Spiritual Pimp Part 2: The Manipulation of Sexual Energy

African Spiritual Systems Study Part 1: Overstanding Yoruba

Visit **www.blogtalkradio.com/ambassadorausar** on the 9th and 19th of every month at 9pm to speak live with **Ambassador Ausar** the host of the hit radio show *Afrikan Holistic Healing* as he builds with the "the family" on the many issues and challenges facing our community.

Contact Ambassador Ausar at
ambassadorausar@gmail.com

Made in the USA
Lexington, KY
09 January 2012